So Great a Cloud of Witnesses:
Heroes from Church History

SELECTED AND EDITED BY
Robert Terry

Coram Deo Academy

Cover: The Charity of St. Elizabeth of Hungary by Edmund Leighton

Back Cover: Icon depicting Constantine I, accompanied by the bishops of the First Council of Nicaea (325), holding the Nicene Creed.

Scripture quotations are from the King James Version

ISBN: 979-8-9857547-0-4

TABLE OF CONTENTS

PREFACE

This book is the product of a several year hunt for short, well-written, and age-appropriate biographies of great men and women from church history. Fortunately, there were a number of quality public domain texts available in English from the pre-World War I era – a high point in literary culture and books for children. The reader may notice a slight emphasis on biographies of Christians living in the British Isles. The authors, for the most part, were British and were writing for an early twentieth century English-speaking audience. Each of the biographies has been lightly edited for length, language, and content. It is my hope that *So Great A Cloud of Witnesses: Heroes from Church History* will inform and inspire many Coram Deo Academy students in the years to come.

Many thanks go to those who helped with this project. First, Mrs. Sarah Colby, CDA parent and board advisor, whose detailed proofing, comments, questions, and suggestions made this a much better book. Thanks also go to other readers who provided feedback: Mrs. Jennifer Southerland, Director of Grammar and Logic Curriculum, Dr. Traci Heitschmidt, History Department Chair, and Wendy Powell, English Department Chair. Cover design, typesetting, and artwork placement was done by Andrew Kendall. This book is more beautiful thanks to his help. Finally, this project would not have been completed without the support of Coram Deo Academy's board and administration; it has been a pleasure to serve the CDA community.

Robert J. Terry
Lewisville, TX
March 2022

INTRODUCTION FOR PARENTS

ROBERT J. TERRY

OVERVIEW

The purpose of *So Great A Cloud of Witnesses: Heroes from Church History* is to introduce Coram Deo Academy's sixth grade students to the lives of great Christians throughout church history. It is my hope that parents too will enjoy the book and read and discuss it with their children. Most of the discussion should center on how the men and women in the book imitate the life of Christ and the Apostles. Though the text intentionally minimizes theological controversy for the sixth-grade reader, the biographies are written by multiple authors from a variety of Christian traditions, covering eighteen centuries of history, so there will be questions and areas of disagreement encountered by many readers. These are also opportunities for discussion between parent and child.

A CHRISTIAN VIEW OF HISTORY

Not only is the Christian God the Lord of history, but He has also acted and entered history as the God-man Christ Jesus. Christ's incarnation, life, death, resurrection, and ascension are at the central point of history and the key to historical understanding. Because Christ is at the center, much of Ancient and Medieval writings of church history have focused on individual lives and specific events and how they exemplify Christ. To modern readers this form of history can seem strange and disconnected. We are more used to a historical focus on cause and effect, development, and political change. The ancients were more interested in how our lives could develop and change to be more Christlike, and therefore biographies or "Saint's Lives" provided exemplars for contemplation and imitation. This book reflects the older approach to history, though it also touches on the larger themes which will be discussed in class: the early persecutions, the spread of the Christian faith through missions, the church's encounter with Islam, and the Protestant Reformation.

A Christian view of history also differs from other historical understandings because there will come a day when history draws to a definitive conclusion. That Christ will return to judge the living and the dead infuses every moment with meaning. What we do in the present has eternal significance.

THE USE OF THE TERM "SAINT"

The term "saint" comes into English from the Latin word, sanctus, meaning one who is set apart for God's service or one who is holy. In the English Standard Version of the Bible, the term "saint" occurs over eighty times in the Old and New

Testaments. In the Scriptures, the word generally refers to members of the church. Here are three examples of its use:

Precious in the sight of the LORD is the death of his saints. (Psalm 116:15)

So that he may establish your hearts blameless in holiness before our God and Father, at the coming of our Lord Jesus with all his saints. (1 Thessalonians 3:13)

And when he had taken the scroll, the four living creatures and the twenty-four elders fell down before the Lamb, each holding a harp, and golden bowls full of incense, which are the prayers of the saints. (Revelation 5:8)

It is therefore appropriate to use the term "saint" for those who are members of Christ's church. In addition to this general use, historically, those who were apostles, martyrs, confessors, or who have shown clearly what it means to follow Christ have been given the honorific title of "Saint." They personally imitated Christ in some significant way and the church sought to remember them. This is the normal meaning and usage of the term in the book. Those who have traditionally been given the title "Saint" have retained that title.

MARTYRDOM AND DEATH

Especially in the early parts of the book, there is a focus on the martyrs. It has been well said that "the blood of the martyrs is the seed of the church." In the fourth century, St. Athanasius was able to appeal to the martyrs and their fearlessness in the face of death as a key proof of the resurrection of Christ. Unlike their pagan neighbors, Christians did not fear death. In all places and times before the modern era, death would have been a normal part of human life. Most people would have seen the dead bodies of family and neighbors at times in their lives. Death would have been an ever-present reality and a cause for Christian reflection. Modern American culture oddly attempts to hide real death from us while showing us uncountable "virtual" deaths on movie and video game screens. We need to restore a Christian attitude toward death.

The lives in the book will typically also include an account of the person's death. Ancient Christians put great importance on the way one met with the end of life. Very few birthdays of great Christians were remembered, but the day of their repose (or death) was recorded and remembered. This practice comes from both Christ's example and words in Matthew 24:13, "But he that shall endure unto the end, the same shall be saved."

A few students may read these accounts and be affected by them enough to require some discussion and counsel. It is a great opportunity to remind them that death, "the last enemy," has been defeated by Christ and that we have hope in the resurrection to come. We need not fear death.

LIVES, LEGENDS, AND HAGIOGRAPHY

Much of ancient and medieval history comes to us from church tradition, chronicles, and hagiography (the lives of the saints). A few of the early lives have little documentary evidence, and occasionally there may be differing accounts of the lives of some saints. Further, it is the nature of a summary or a children's history book that complex matters be simplified, and to simplify history is to distort it however mildly. That being said, these are some of the most important lives that Christian people have preserved for us to remember.

Some of the lives include miracles and fantastic elements. The miraculous cannot be established or disproved by a modern scientific approach to history or any other approach. We also were not witnesses to the events. I believe the best practice is to be open to the miraculous and not pass judgment on the miracles recorded in church history; then we avoid either becoming skeptics or overly credulous.

Several of the stories in the book are legends and are stated as such in the text: St. George and the Dragon, St. Christopher, and some of the stories about St. Bridget of Kildare fall into this category. These are included because of their importance to Christians of the time, but also because these stories continue to influence art and literature today. Sometimes the legendary stories are the best kinds of stories to bring out an eternal truth.

MONKS AND MONASTICISM

Many of the lives contained in the book concern monastics, both monks and nuns, which is a world quite foreign to many modern Christians. The monastic movement was an important place for those who sought to live the life of Christ in an intense way, ordering all of life around prayer, worship, and work. Monasteries were also centers for ministering to non-monastics though the dispensing of spiritual counsel, care of the poor and sick, and holding up an ideal to the organized church. Monasteries also preserved the tradition of learning through history. The work of monastics in missions, teaching, and preaching can hardly by overstated.

CONCLUSION

It is my sincere desire that *So Great A Cloud of Witnesses: Heroes from Church History* will kindle your student's passion to learn more about the many great men and women in church history and to be inspired toward a greater imitation of Christ!

The Church, by Its Martyrs, Overcomes the World

John Mason Neale

The history of the Church properly begins at the Day of Pentecost. For then it was that the Apostles were filled with the Holy Spirit, that they might go and teach all nations. But I shall pass quickly over those events, which you may read for yourselves in the Book of Acts.

It is believed that our Lord commanded His Apostles to remain together in Jerusalem for twelve years. And so we read that, in the persecution which arose after the death of Stephen, they that believed "were scattered abroad, except the Apostles."[1] The Twelve stayed on in that city, till the time came at which they were to part, never to meet again in this world.

In the Acts you read of the chief things, which happened in these twelve years. St. Stephen, the first Martyr, and St. James the Apostle, glorified God by laying down their lives; Saul was

---

1   Acts 8:1

1

called from being a blasphemer and persecutor, and injurious, to be Saint Paul, the Great Apostle. And by degrees the Apostles, being led by the Holy Spirit into all truth, learned that the Gospel was to be preached to the Gentiles also, and not, as they at first thought, to the Jews only. The first who did this were some disciples of the island of Cyprus, and of Cyrene in Egypt, when they fled to Antioch after the martyrdom of St. Stephen. But the first to whom God made manifest His Will in this matter was St. Peter, in the vision of the great sheet let down from Heaven, of which you may read in the tenth chapter of the Acts. Afterwards, indeed, St. Paul became the chief Apostle of the Gentiles, and labored more abundantly than they all; yet not he, but the Grace of God that was with him.

St. Peter was first the Bishop of Antioch: after that he went to Rome, where the emperor then lived, who ruled the greater part of the world. From there he sent St. Mark into Egypt, where he founded the Church of Alexandria. Of St. Paul's journeys you read in the Acts. St. John went into Asia Minor and was Bishop of Ephesus. St. Thomas travelled into India; some say to China also. St. Bartholomew labored in Armenia. St. Matthew preached in Ethiopia; so also did St. Matthias. St. Simon the Canaanite, and St. Jude, went to Mesopotamia, Persia, and Arabia. St. Philip lived in Phrygia. St. Andrew proclaimed Christ in Russia and Greece. According to tradition, all of the

Apostles, except St. John, finished their lives by martyrdom, and so they entered into the joy of their Lord. There they now are waiting for the day when they shall sit on twelve thrones, judging kindreds, and nations, and people.

At first, it was God's good will that for some time the Church should not suffer any great persecution. Tiberius was the Roman Emperor when our Lord was crucified; but he, and those who came after him, Caligula and Claudius, let the Christians remain in peace. Nero, who succeeded Claudius, and who became a monster of wickedness, left them to themselves for ten years. In the meanwhile, St. Matthew, St. Mark, and St. Luke, had written their Gospels, and St. Paul, most of his epistles. By this time also, in Asia Minor, Palestine, Egypt, Syria, Greece, and Italy, many bishops had been consecrated by the Apostles; some of them we find mentioned in the New Testament, as Timothy and Titus.

St. Luke tells us in the Acts how St. Paul appealed to Caesar, that is, to Nero, and so was sent by Festus, the Roman Governor of Judea, to Rome. After remaining there more than two years, in his own hired house, he was set at liberty. Then he went into France, where he is said to have consecrated some bishops, by whose preaching and labors the Gospel spread over that country. From France he journeyed into Spain; and some say that he even went to England. After this he returned into the East.

"THE SEPARATION OF THE APOSTLES."—FROM A PICTURE BY CHARLES GLEYRE.

"THE SEPARATION OF THE APOSTLES."
BY C. GLEYRE.

THE subject of this picture is the figurative separation of the Apostles at the foot of the Cross, when they went forth into all lands preaching the gospel. M. Gleyre, the artist, has shown considerable skill and taste in the composition, the result being a highly-effective and striking group, well calculated to enforce the sentiment intended, namely, the importance of the apostolic mission as based upon, and springing from, the cross. For the rest, as in the attitudes, the disposition of the draperies, and the studied simplicity of the landscape, the treatment is peculiarly French, and the picture may be taken as a fair average specimen of the modern French scriptural school. Our Engraving is copied, by permission, from a fine print, after the picture, by Gautin, published by Messrs. Gambard and Co.

St. James Confesses Christ and Suffers Martyrdom, AD 62

John Mason Neale

All this time St. James the Just had been bishop of the Church at Jerusalem. Now there began to be signs that the fearful cry of the mob that demanded Jesus's crucifixion, "His blood be on us and on our children,"[2] was about to be fulfilled. At last, one Ananus, a Sadducee, was made High Priest; and he filled up the measure of the iniquities of his people. He called together the chief priests and elders and gave orders that James should be set before them. This was at the time of the Passover, and multitudes of the Jews had come up to keep the feast. "We know," said the High Priest, "how much the people honor and reverence you: you know also how they err, forsaking the Law of Moses, and following Jesus, which was called Christ. Wherefore it is fit that you should go up to the top of the Temple, whence you can be heard of the multi-

---

2   Matthew 27:25

tude, and tell them how grievously they are in error touching that deceiver." "I will go up there," said St. James, "and will speak to the people." Accordingly, he went up to the top of the Temple; and there, from the height of its terrace, glittering with snow-white marble, he looked down on the vast multitude that rolled here and there below him, and struggled onwards to hear his words. "Tell us, O Just one," cried the Pharisees, "what this people is to think of Jesus of Nazareth, Whom they ignorantly worship?" "Why ask ye me," said St. James, "touching Christ the Son of Man? He now sitteth on the right hand of God, and shall come again with glory, to judge the living and the dead." The multitude cried, as with one voice, "Hosanna to the Son of David!" But the Scribes said, "It was ill done to give this man's testimony concerning Christ. The Just one hath grievously erred." And hurrying to the roof of the Temple, they threw St. James down among the people. Still, however, he lived, and with his remaining strength, kneeling, he said, "Lord God, lay not this sin to their charge." A man of the house of the Rechabites (you will remember God's promise made to them by the Prophet Jeremiah[3]) cried, "What do ye? The Just one prays for you." But a fuller[4], who stood by, struck the holy Apostle on the head

---

3   Jeremiah 35:18-19

4   A fuller is someone who works with wool in the production of clothing.

with a mallet; and he thus entered into the joy of his Lord. In his place the Church of Jerusalem chose Simeon, the son of Cleophas (and thus a relation of our Lord according to the flesh), to be their bishop.

NOS AUTEM
PRÆDICAMUS
CHRISTUM
CRUCIFIXUM
··· 1°·COR·I·23·

R. DE CRAMER

St. Peter & St. Paul, AD 65

John Mason Neale

And now there appeared in the city, at the Feast of Tabernacles, a man named Jesus[5], the son of Ananus. He stood in the Temple, and cried continually, "A voice from the east! A voice from the west! A voice from the four winds against Jerusalem! A voice against the Temple and the people! A voice against the bridegroom and the bride!" He was persecuted, laughed at, imprisoned, scourged till the bones were laid bare, but still he uttered not a syllable save this doleful cry. At last they let him go; and he wandered up and down the streets, perpetually repeating, "A voice from the east! A voice from the west!" but oftener, and more sadly, at the time of the principal feasts.

There were other dreadful signs. At nine o'clock in the evening, at the Feast of the Passover, the altar of burnt offerings was surrounded with such a light that the Temple and the

---

5   This is not Jesus the Christ.

court shone as at mid-day. The great eastern door, which was of brass, and so heavy that it required twenty men to move it, opened of its own accord. In the month of May, at sunset, the sky seemed full of chariots and horses and armies of fire. And at the Feast of Pentecost, when the priests went into the Temple, they heard the sound as of footsteps leaving the place, and then a terrible voice that said, "Let us depart hence!" But before I tell you of the destruction of Jerusalem, I must say something of the first persecution.

The first persecution, under Nero, A.D. 64 the Emperor Nero, who, as I said, was a monster of wickedness, in the month of July, set fire to the city of Rome. This he did that he might enjoy the sight, and be able to rebuild the city in a more stately manner. Notwithstanding the care he took to keep his secret, he was suspected of being the author of the fire; and so, to turn people's thoughts from himself, he accused the Christians of the crime. Of those early Roman and Italian martyrs we read very little. We only know that some were given to the wild beasts, others covered with the skins of deer, and so torn in pieces by dogs; some were smeared over with pitch, and being then fastened to posts in the streets, were set light to, and served as torches. In those first years, the Christians, not foreseeing the fiery trial that was to try them for so long a time, were not so careful to preserve the "Acts of the Martyrs" as they afterwards were; so that the names of those who suffered under Nero, though long since written in the Book of Life, are but little known to us.

But of two glorious confessors we do know. St. Peter seems to have been some time at Rome, and now St. Paul came there also. Both felt that they were soon to finish their course. St. Peter says, "Knowing that I must shortly put off this my tabernacle; even as our Lord Jesus Christ hath showed me."[6] St. Paul says, "I have fought a good fight, I have finished my course, I have kept the faith: henceforth there is laid up for me a Crown of Righteousness."[7] They were thrown into the Mamertine prison, a dark, noisome dungeon, which remains to this day; and this was the reason.

Simon the magician—who had bewitched the people of Samaria, giving out that he was some great one, and who had afterwards sought to buy the power of working miracles—had all his life long been doing what he could to hurt the Church of God by his false signs. He had come to Rome, and became a favorite of Nero, who was fond of studying magic. He showed the Emperor several great wonders by the power of the devil, and at last promised to fly. The day having come, Nero, and a vast crowd, gathered together to see this strange miracle.

---

6   2 Peter 1:14
7   2 Timothy 4:7-8

Simon came forward, and presently rose towards the sky. The Apostles, Peter and Paul, were there; and they knelt down, and called on the Name of Jesus Christ. At the same moment the magician fell to the ground, and broke both his legs. He was carried into a house; and there, mad with his pain and shame, he ended his life.

Nero was enraged, and more particularly against St. Paul, who had before this converted one of the Emperor's favorite concubines. The Apostles were therefore, as I said, thrown into the Mamertine prison, where they remained nine months. Here they converted forty-seven prisoners, and besides these the two jailers, Processus and Martinianus, who afterwards became glorious martyrs. At last the Christians persuaded St. Peter to leave the prison and flee. He went forth by night; but as he was going out of the gate of the city, he beheld our Lord, as he had known Him in the flesh, entering in. St. Peter said, "Lord, where goest Thou?" And the Lord answered, "I go to be crucified again in Rome." And having so said, He vanished from his sight. This St. Peter understood to be a prophecy of his own martyrdom; and he therefore returned to the prison. Shortly after this, his wife was led to death. He congratulated her on going home first, and said, "Woman, remember the Lord."

On the 29th of June, the two glorious Apostles were led forth to martyrdom. St. Paul, as being a Roman citizen, was beheaded. It was at a place called Salviennae, three miles from the city, and on his way there he converted three soldiers, who afterwards became martyrs. St. Peter was taken to the Janiculan Hill, the part of Rome where the Jews lived, and there crucified. He prayed that it might be with his head downwards, because, he said, "I am not worthy to suffer as my Master did."

THE JEWISH WAR BEGINS, AD 66

JOHN MASON NEALE

Leaving these two most blessed Apostles in the glory of their Lord, I must go on to a sad story, and tell you about the Jewish war. Florus was now the governor of Judea, and as he was very cruel, and exacted money by the most unjust means, the Jews at last broke out into open rebellion. Roman forces poured in from all quarters against them; and at length the Governor of Syria, Cestius Gallus, led his army to Jerusalem. He might have taken it at once, but he was persuaded that he had not enough soldiers, and therefore retreated. The Jews pursued, and cut off a great number of his men.

Now doubtless God ordered this, that the Christians might have the opportunity of escaping from the miserable city. For when they saw the standards of the Roman army, on which idols were set, arrayed round the walls, they called to mind the words of our Lord, "When ye therefore shall see the abomination of desolation, spoken of by Daniel the Prophet, standing in the Holy Place (whoso readeth, let him understand), then let them which be in Judea flee unto the mountains."[8] When, therefore, the army of Cestius Gallus retreated, the Christians, led by St. Simeon, their bishop, left Jerusalem, and fled to Pella, a city in the mountains, and not one of them perished in the war.

Then followed that siege, which perhaps is the most dreadful thing in history. The Jews were shut up in Jerusalem by Vespasian, the Roman General. But though the enemy was daily attacking the walls, though the machines battered the ramparts, and flung huge rocks into the streets, the miserable Jews were divided into two parties, and daily fighting with each other. The two leaders, both bloodthirsty tyrants, were named John and Simon[9]. One held the upper and one the lower part of the city. So there was war without, and all kind of bloodshed, treachery, and cruelty within. Still the people believed that the God of Abraham, Isaac, and Jacob, would not forsake His people. They were infatuated to their destruction; and though the Romans offered them terms of peace, they resolved to hold out to the last. And all this while they were plotting and fighting against each other; and the Temple itself was polluted with murder.

---

8   Matthew 24:15-16

9   Not to be confused with the Apostles John and Simon Peter.

When the siege was formed, it was the time of the Passover. A vast multitude of strangers were therefore shut up in the city. And soon famine—the most dreadful famine we read of—began. Then were fulfilled the curses written in the twenty-eighth chapter of Deuteronomy. When provisions failed, men ate, first, horses; then mice, rats, and other vermin; then straps, leather, and skins; then filth of all kinds. Multitudes died daily. Many tried to give themselves up to the Romans; but they were not allowed to come forth. When any, the vilest food was found, men fought for it as for a treasure.

Vespasian was now Emperor; but his son Titus, a very gentle prince, carried on the siege, and with tears called God to witness that the Jews, and not he, were the authors of this misery. All this time, Jesus the son of Ananus went round with his doleful cry; but now the words were — "Woe! Woe to the city! — Woe! Woe to the people! — Woe! Woe to the Temple!" At last, as he was on the walls, he suddenly cried out — "Woe! Woe to myself also!" and almost at the same moment a stone from one of the engines slew him.

Every day the famine grew more terrible; every day the Romans advanced further and further; every day murders and fights in the city increased. But still the Jews believed that God would save them. Titus was very anxious to spare the Temple. But in an assault on the tenth of August, the same day on which it had been burnt by Nebuchadnezzar, it was set fire to, and destroyed, and all within it put to the sword.

Titus, having offered sacrifice on the ground where the Temple had stood, now pressed on the siege. Still the Jews fortified themselves on Mount Zion; till on Saturday, September 8th, the place was taken by assault. The city was all but destroyed, and the ground was ploughed up. In the siege, eleven hundred thousand Jews perished; and after it, ninety-seven thousand were sold as captives. And thus the dreadful prayer was fulfilled: "His Blood be on us, and on our children."[10]

Two years before the destruction of Jerusalem, Nero's wickedness had become too great to be borne. A conspiracy was formed against him; he fled from Rome and killed himself. After a short reign of three Emperors—Galba, Otho, and Vitellius— Vespasian, as I told you, was elected Emperor by the soldiers.

---

10   Matthew 27:25

St. John the Apostle, AD 99

John Mason Neale

Titus succeeded Vespasian: but he soon died; and then his brother Domitian became Emperor. He was almost as cruel as Nero, but it was not till nearly the end of his reign, A.D. 95, that he began the second persecution.

St. John the Apostle was now at Rome. When he refused to sacrifice to idols, he was condemned to be put into a vessel of boiling oil: but it did him no harm. The Apostle was then banished to Patmos, an island of the Aegean Sea, where he beheld the visions, which he wrote in the Book of Revelation. Of other Martyrs in this persecution we know very little. But I must tell you something more of the last days of St. John.

Domitian was murdered in 96; and Nerva, who succeeded him, pardoned all those who had been banished. St. John then went to Ephesus. Here the Christians asked him to write a Gospel, for fearful heresies were beginning to creep in among them,

according to that saying of St. Paul, "I know that after my departure shall grievous wolves enter in among you, not sparing the flock."[11] The chief teachers of these were called Ebion and Cerinthus: they said that Jesus Christ was not really and truly God: in part they observed the Jewish law; and in part they mixed with it a kind of horrible acknowledgment of the devil.

When, therefore, the Christians of Ephesus and the bishops of that part of Asia besought the Apostle to write a Gospel which should set forth the True Faith as to our Lord's Godhead, he requested them to keep a fast three days: and then, as if desiring to crush down all the heresies concerning our Lord that would afterwards infest the Church, he begins his Gospel: In the beginning was the Word, and the Word was with God, and the Word was God.[12] While at Ephesus he also wrote his three epistles.[13]

I will tell you a story of what he did there. Going for a time, as his custom was, to see the Christians in a city not far off, he found a young man for whom he felt a strong love. He recommended him to the bishop of the place as a charge for which he should answer in the day of Jesus Christ. The bishop took the young man to his own house, and after some time baptized him.

---

11   Acts 20:29

12   John 1:1

13   Those epistles (letters) are in the New Testament: 1 John, 2 John, 3 John.

Some years after, the Apostle came again to the same city. "Where," asked he of the bishop, "is the young man whom I committed to your charge?" "He is dead," said the bishop, casting down his eyes. "Is he indeed dead?" inquired St. John. "He is dead in trespasses and sins," replied the other. Then the whole sad account came out; that this young man had fallen into evil company and sinful ways, and going on from bad to worse, was now the chief of a band of robbers who infested the mountains nearby. St. John called for a horse and a guide, went to the mountains, and was taken, as he wished, by the thieves. "Carry me to your leader!" he said. They did so. When the young man saw the Apostle, he trembled exceedingly, and would fain[14] have fled. "What, my son!" cried St. John; "would you flee from an unarmed old man and your father? Return with me, and fear not; there is hope yet: I have obtained forgiveness for you from our Lord Jesus Christ."[15] Thus he persuaded the leader of the robbers to return to the city, and never left him till he had seen him restored, as a true penitent, to the fold.

When St. John was very old, he used to be carried to the assembly of the Christians, and to say these words, "Little children, love one another."[16] At length his disciples asked, "Why,

14   Willingly
15   John 20:23
16   1 John 3:18

O Master, dost thou so often say the same words?" "Because," he answered, "it is the command of Jesus Christ; and if ye fulfil it, it sufficeth." At last he fell asleep in the Lord, and was buried near Ephesus (A.D. 99).

The Manner *in which* IGNATIUS, Bishop *of* Antioch, *was torn to pieces by* WILD BEASTS *by order of the* Romans.

St. Ignatius of Antioch, AD 107

Jetta Wolff

"At the same time came the disciples unto Jesus, saying, Who is the greatest in the kingdom of heaven? And Jesus called a little child unto Him, and set him in the midst of them, and said, Verily I say unto you, Except ye be converted, and become as little children, ye shall not enter into the kingdom of heaven. Whosoever therefore shall humble himself as this little child, the same is greatest in the kingdom of heaven."[17]

You have probably heard this story before. Perhaps you have also read it for yourselves in your Testament. Have you never thought that you would like to know what became of this little child, how he grew up, and what he did when a man?

We can never be quite sure about it, but from very early times it has been believed that a good and holy man named Ignatius Theophorus was that little child. Theophorus is a

---

17   Matthew 18:1-3

Greek word and means one who bears God in his heart; and from all that is known of the life of the holy man, it does seem truly as if, from the time that Jesus laid His hands on him in Capernaum and led him before the disciples as an example of innocence, the Spirit of Christ had always dwelt with him. He was brought up among the Apostles, and the blessed St. John, the Apostle of Divine love, took chief charge of him.

It is most likely that Ignatius went about with St. John until he was more than thirty years of age. Then he was sent to a church at Antioch to care for and govern it. It was at Antioch, you know, that those who believed in Christ were first called Christians.[18] This was then a nick-name—a name given in scorn.

The people of the city laughed and jeered at all who followed the teaching of our Savior, and as they were fond of giving people nick-names, they chose this—the name we are now most proud to bear—for the believers on Jesus Christ.

St. Ignatius ruled the Church he was set over with love and wisdom. He was always calm and gentle—full of love. He was very fond of music, and he taught the Christians to sing hymns in the services and showed them how to chant the psalms in the way we now chant them in so many of our churches—antiphonally—that is, some of the singers standing on one side of the choir, some on the other, and each side singing a verse in turn.

_____

18   Acts 11:26

Ignatius had been at Antioch for almost fifty years, and was quite an old man, when one day there was a great earthquake in the city. Its walls shook and toppled over, the houses fell, many people were killed, and all they had was destroyed.

There was fear on all sides. Then the pagans said the earthquake had been sent by their gods, who were angry that so many of the people here and everywhere had become Christians. And they said many false, cruel things about the Christians and tried to make men believe that they were bad, wicked people who would do all the ill they could to those around them.

Now, Trajan, who was Emperor of Rome at this time, and who had power over lands in many parts of the world, had wished to be kind to the Christians, and had tried to let no harm come to them. But when his people came and told him of the great fear they were in through the earthquake, and how all men thought it had come upon them on account of this "new sect," as they called the followers of our Savior, then he did not dare to go on being kind—he feared to make the people too much enraged against him.

Ignatius, who knew of all this, left Antioch, and went and stood before the great Emperor. He said he had come to prove how false was all that had been said about the Christians.

Trajan was staying in the East at this time and was not very far from Antioch. He was seated upon a grand chair of state, and had soldiers and officers of his court around him when St. Ignatius was brought in. Calm and firm the old man, with his gentle eyes and his pure, noble face, stood before the Emperor.

But Trajan looked at him in anger, called him an evil demon, and demanded who he was that he dared to go against his laws, and to cause his fellowmen to perish.

The Bishop gave his name, "Ignatius Theophorus." Names in those days always had some special meaning. Trajan at once asked why he was called "Theophorus."

"Theophorus is one who bears God in his heart," replied Ignatius.

"What dost thou mean by God?" cried the Emperor.

Then Ignatius spoke of Jesus, the crucified Savior, and of the kingdom of God in the heart of man.

When the Emperor heard St. Ignatius speak thus, he fell into a great rage; for although he had not wished to be cruel to the Christians, he hated to think of Jesus as God. So, he ordered the aged saint to be bound and carried to Rome, there to be torn to death by wild beasts at a great show that was held each year.

St. Ignatius was not at all sad when he heard this. He thought it a joy to die for the sake of Christ; he even helped to fasten on his own chains. Then some soldiers took charge of him, and he was sent on his way to Rome. But they did not take him by the most direct road. It has been thought that because

Trajan was not really a cruel man at heart, he did try after all to save the old saint from so dreadful a death. He sent him by a long, round-about way to Rome, thinking, perhaps, that when the people saw the white-haired old man led in chains through their land, and about to be put to a cruel death in their midst, they might feel some pity, and save him at the last.

Poor old man! But he showed no sign of grief. Through his whole life, since the very day no doubt that Christ had laid His hands on him, he had kept his sweet joyous temper, and he did not change in the least now. Through all the journey his face was bright and glad.

He was kept some time at a place called Smyrna, in Asia Minor. Here there were Christian churches, and though St. Ignatius was closely guarded, and chained to the wrist of a soldier whenever he went out, he was allowed to go about a little, and to see the friends who could come to him there. A great many came. They loved him so truly as to be ready to risk much to go and comfort him in his trial. So, they came in spite of the pagans who were in charge of the saint, and who were full of hatred for them and him.

While he was kept thus at Smyrna, St. Ignatius wrote many letters or epistles to the Churches of Asia. These letters have always been kept with great care by the Church, and so they have come down to our own day, and we can read now the very words the good old saint wrote to the Christian people of those times. They are beautiful letters, very like the epistles which we have in the New Testament from St. Paul and St. John.

After a while an order came that Ignatius must go on to Rome. The guards then took him on board ship again. They sailed away, but still they did not travel very fast, and they stopped at two or three places as they came to them. Everywhere those who had known and loved St. Ignatius came out to greet him.

Many prayed him to let them go to the Emperor and beg that his life might be spared. But the old man would not hear of this. To die for the faith of Christ was to him the highest honor.

The great feast and fair was already going on in Rome when Ignatius reached the city. The streets were full of people, shouting, dancing, joking, and looking at shows and sports. But they were still waiting for what they thought would be the finest sport of all—the death of the Christian saint.

In a great round building called an amphitheater were rows of seats, one row raised behind the other, making a circle round a large open space, where wild beasts were in those days set to fight with each other and with men.

Here Ignatius was to be led to meet his death. Friends had come with him for the last few miles of his journey; their love had been his comfort: his blessing, the last blessing of their beloved and holy Bishop, was now to comfort them. Then they took their leave, and he was led under one of the low, dark archways into the amphitheater.

The open space in which these fearful combats took place was always strewn over with sand; it was called the "arena," which means "sand-covered."

Many were the horrible fights which took place here between men and beasts, but the sight was looked on in those days as fine sport. Men fought with the wild beasts till their strength was spent; then an appeal would be made to the people seated around. If they wished the lives of the men to be spared, they would raise their thumbs—this was the sign of mercy; if no sign were made, the fight was to go on till death. Such was the custom for those trained on purpose for these combats—the men called "gladiators." St. Ignatius was not a gladiator, but a victim, a Christian led to martyrdom, for him there was to be no thought of mercy or pity.

Fresh sand had been strewn in the arena, and as the old man was led there, he heard the roaring of the lions in the dens below. A moment more and they were out upon him—two fierce lions. In a few seconds all that was left in this world of the noble old man was a handful of bones: "But the souls of the righteous are in the hand of God; there shall no torment touch them."[19]

---

19   Book of Wisdom 3:1 (a deuterocanonical book considered part of the Old Testament by Roman Catholics, Eastern Orthodox, and Oriental Orthodox Christians.)

Coelitus ô regni me fac consistere portu,
Neu cadat à venti vi superata ratis.

St. Polycarp of Smyrna, AD 166

Jetta Wolff

There is another "Father of the Church" who is thought also to have been taught by St. John. His name was Polycarp, which means "much fruit." He did truly bear much and precious fruit for the Church of Christ.

It is said that Polycarp was at first a slave, and that a good Greek lady, called Callista, took him to live in her house, had him taught, and then gave him his freedom. He showed great talent and ceased not to study and to work. By-and-by he was made a deacon and worked for some years under the Bishop of Smyrna. Then, many years later, about the time that St. Ignatius was put to death, Polycarp became himself Bishop of Smyrna.

He dwelt there for many years, preaching and teaching, carrying out with faithfulness and love all the duties of his office. During all this time he wrote to the other Churches of Asia letters full of devoted affection and earnest, helpful thought. He believed he should die a martyr; he fain[20] would follow in the path of the Apostles, and he counted it a glory to give up his life for his faith. But he grew to old age, and it was a time of peace for the Christians.

Then all at once things changed. Famine, war, plague came upon the empire of Rome, and again men said it was on account of the Christians that the land was so greatly troubled. The fury of the people was allowed to burst out upon them; many were taken and brought before the tribunal. When they refused to give up their faith, they were put to death with horrible cruelty. The friends of Polycarp begged him to go away from the city, and hide from the anger of the people, in a little country place within reach. He knew it was not right to seek death, though he felt sure he would soon be called upon to give up his life for Christ. So, he went away to the secluded village. But the direction he had taken was found out, and in order to discover exactly where the Christian bishop lay hidden, the persecutors got hold of two children from the village. They beat the poor little boys and tried to frighten them into saying where they must look to come upon St. Polycarp. One child was strong and firm; he bravely bore the beating; he was ready to die under the cruel blows rather than betray the bishop. The other could not hold out. So, when the

---

20   With pleasure; gladly.

searchers knew where to find their prey they sent a body of horsemen, who placed themselves round the bishop's dwelling. "The Lord's will be done," said the old man, as he gave himself up. They mounted him upon an ass, and early in the morning set out for the city.

Some of the great men of the place begged him to give in—to bow down before the gods of the heathen. At first Polycarp would not even answer such a proposition; but when they went on pressing him, he said firmly, "I shall never do what you ask." At this they were very angry, and pushed rudely by him, so that he fell and hurt his leg.

He was led into the great amphitheater: it was full of people. When the judge saw the fine old man stand there, quite calm and gentle, unmoved before the mass of gaping lookers on, he was much struck, and was sorry to think he would have to give him up to death. So he, too, began to beg St. Polycarp to deny Christ.

"Eighty and six years have I served Him," Polycarp replied; "nor hath He ever done me wrong. Why, then, should I deny my King and Saviour?"

"Knowest thou not," said the judge, "that I have beasts to which I will cast thee if thou yieldest not?"

"Let them come," said Polycarp. I will not turn from good to evil, but from evil to good it is well to pass."

"If thou carest not for the beasts, thou shalt be burnt with fire," cried the judge.

"Thou dost threaten me with a flame that is soon burnt out," said Polycarp. "Delay not, bring whatever thou wilt."

Then the people cried out, "Away with him! the beasts for Polycarp!"

But the beast shows were over. They cried, "Fire," and men hurried off to bring kindling. A stake was piled, and the aged saint was placed upon it. It was the custom at Smyrna to fasten victims to the stake with nails. Polycarp would not let this be done for him.

Leave me alone," he said, "He Who gives me strength to endure the flames, will enable me to stand firm on the pile of wood." So, they only tied his hands behind.

As the fire was set light to, Polycarp began to sing words of praise to God. We have the very words of this hymn still; it is one of the oldest hymns which have come down to us. Thus singing, the noble old man stood among the flames. But they did not touch him. A strong wind had risen; the tongues of fire were blown outwards and made a sort of arch all-round the saint, leaving him unharmed in their midst. At this sight the people only grew the more enraged and called out to one who was near to kill the old man at once. A moment later a short sword was plunged into his left side. Then the boy was ordered to be burnt—the brave child who had stood so firm under torture, who had been ready to bear any pain rather than betray the Christian bishop to his enemies: "Baptized in blood for Jesus' sake."[21]

It was Easter Eve, April 25th, 166. At night some of the Christians crept back to the blackened pile and took away what they could find of the bones of their beloved bishop. They buried them on the hillside near, and there stands to this day a small Christian church over the spot.

---

21   From John Keble's poem "The Holy Innocents."

Saint Symphorien, par Ingres.

ST. SYMPHORIAN, AD 178

JETTA WOLFF

There were many more brave men and women who suffered death for their faith about this time. Wherever there was a Christian Church—in Italy, Gaul, Greece, or Britain, it was all the same—men were called on to deny or suffer. To one young man, named Symphorian, of high birth, great things were promised, if only he would worship the Roman gods. But he was firm: he scorned the temptation. Then the judge said he must be beheaded. As he walked along outside the city, led by soldiers to his death, there was heard a cry from the walls, "My son!"

The soldiers stopped. Looking up, they saw the mother of the young man gazing down upon him. What a moment! But no, it was not in weak sorrow that the mother called her boy. Listen to the words she spoke:

"My son, remember the living God, and stand fast to the

end. Lift up thy heart and look to Him Who is King in the heavens. Fear not; they will not take thy life this day, they will but change it for the better one."

Were not these grand last words to hear from his mother?

Bravely then the young man knelt and bowed his head to the stroke of the sword. He was buried near the spot where he died, and in after times a church was built over the place where he was believed to lie.

St. Irenaeus of Lyons, AD 202

Jetta Wolff

There is yet one other great and noble Greek Father of the Church about whom I must tell you something. His name was Irenaeus, which means "peaceful;" and I think through all the storms and trials of his life he must indeed have kept the peace of God in his heart.

He was a very learned man and was sent by the Church in Asia to preach and work in Gaul. He could at first speak no language but Greek, but in order to be able to teach the faith of Christ to the people of Gaul he worked hard till he could speak Celtic quite well, and so talk to the Gauls and teach them in their own tongue.

This was a very brave thing to do, for it must have given him much trouble and taken up a great deal of his time. But it won for him the love of the people of the land: they were proud that the Christian priest should care to learn their language,

instead of thinking they ought to learn to understand his, which was what many others thought at that time. Among the richer classes in Gaul, Latin and Greek were very commonly spoken; Irenaeus might have considered he was doing his duty in preaching to those alone who could understand the language he was used to speak: that he should stoop to learn the speech of the poor and lowly touched all hearts.

He did a great work in Gaul, and it was through him that the town of Lyons, in the south of France, became a Christian city.

But suddenly there came a terrible end to all the saint's missionary labors. It was a time of cruel persecution. Men were paid to hunt out the Christians and kill them wherever they were to be found. There were very many now in Lyons; without mercy the Roman hirelings fell upon them, killing right and left. Thousands were slain—there was not a single Christian spared. The priest perished among his people.

There is an old church at Lyons, called the Church of St. Irenaeus, where is to be seen an ancient Roman pavement on which are inscribed some Latin verses, saying that 19,000 Christians were killed at the time of this slaughter.

"This is the dawn of infant faith;
The day will follow soon,
When hope shall breathe with fuller breath,

And morn be lost in noon.

"For to the seed that's sown to-day

A harvest-time is given,

When charity with faith to stay

Shall make on earth a heaven."[22]

---

22   From the hymn "Gone is the hollow, murky night" by T. Doubleday.

St. Perpetua, AD 202

Mrs. Molesworth

Among all the martyr stories of ancient or later days, St. Perpetua's is one of the most interesting, for we have all the details of it, up to the very night before her death, related in the saint's own simple, yet dignified, words. Is it not marvelous to think, that across this long stretch of over eighteen hundred years, sweet Perpetua's account of her own sufferings and noble courage, written by herself in her prison, should have been preserved? Not that she praises herself or seems to think there was anything wonderful in her holy heroism. She ascribes all her strength to her dear Lord's goodness, and through all the horrors of her dreadful imprisonment is never weary of thanking and praising her Master.

Vivia Perpetua, to give her full name, was a young married lady, living with her family at Carthage, in Africa. Her mother and brothers were Christians, but not her father. Nor

do we know if her husband was a Christian; it is only said that he was a wealthy and respected man. She had one dear little baby, whom she tenderly loved. Her youngest brother of seven had died just before the persecution broke out. This child had suffered from a very painful disease, and his death was evidently a great grief to his sister, for she relates how, in the prison, she had a wonderful dream about this little boy, which shows how much he was in her thoughts. But except for this sorrow it seems as if Vivia Perpetua's life had been a very happy one. She was young, rich, and beautiful, surrounded by friends who loved her dearly; it is said that her father cared for her most of all his children. There does not seem much in such a life to prepare one for a martyr's death. But the true martyr spirit was in this fair young lady, as firm and fervent as in the strong soldier St. George, or the tried and experienced Clement — as humbly faithful and self-forgetting as in the poor slave Felicitas, who suffered with her.

We know no particulars of the beginning of this persecution, or what directed it to Carthage, and especially to this rich and important family. Perpetua's account begins when already in prison. She tells how for some days she and her companions — two young slaves, Revocatus and Felicitas (probably his sister), two young men, most likely of high rank, Saturninus and Secundulus— were arrested on suspicion of being Christians, shut up for some days in a house, under a strong guard, and then taken to one of the dreadful Roman prisons, where, she says, "I was shocked at the horror and darkness of the place, never having known what such places were." No wonder, for these prisons were dismal holes, with no windows, only a very small opening high up in the wall for the light to come in by. The heat also, she says, was fearful, and the rudeness of the soldiers very hard to bear. In the house, their first quarters, they had been joined by Saturus, whom Perpetua speaks of as her brother. He gave himself up in order to comfort and instruct the others, for he was a learned as well as a holy man, and he arranged that they should all be baptized, as they had not yet received baptism. Perpetua's worst trouble at first was the thought of her poor baby, but two Christian deacons who were allowed to see the prisoners, managed to have the little fellow brought to her, which made her happier, though she was obliged to send him back to her mother to be taken care of. Another terrible trial to her was the visits of her old father, who came constantly entreating her to renounce her faith — "for the sake of his grey hairs to take pity on him." He kissed her hands and her feet with many tears, and she, "full of pain and grieved at heart," yet had strength to repeat that she not give up her Master. "I cannot call myself other than a Christian," she had already said to him at the first, and she touched a pitcher which happened to stand beside her. Can I call this else but a pitcher, which it is?" And he answered, "No." "Nor can I say of myself that I am not what I am — a Christian," she repeated. She had some wonderful and mysteriously beautiful dreams in the prison, which comforted her and the others greatly. Her brother, too, had a vision, which made them feel sure that they were soon to die, while it opened heaven and its blessedness to their faithful eyes.

At last came the day so terrible to these poor people as human beings, so glorious as the followers of their Lord. The slave Felicitas had a little baby, too, even younger and more tender than the Lady Perpetua's infant son. It must have been a bitter sorrow to both these young mothers to have to say good-bye to their children. One would like to know what became of them; one could hope that they grew up Christians worthy of the name and of their noble mothers. I do not want to say too much about the actual sufferings of these martyrs: it is very terrible and heartrending. They were first forced to fight with wild beasts, but none of them were killed in this combat. Perpetua and Felicitas were exposed to a wild cow, who tossed them both. Perpetua, as soon as she came to her senses, raised herself and tried to bind up her long hair, not wishing "to seem forlorn in what was her hour of victory." Then, looking round and seeing her poor slave friend in worse case than herself, she tenderly tried to support her. And even the hard hearts of the brutalized spectators were a little touched. They called out that it was enough; the victims might now be dispatched by the sword. So they were led away to the gate of the arena. And then, it is related, Perpetua seemed to awake out of sleep. She had been stunned, doubtless, by the shock of her cruel fall, and we may also believe that in God's love for His noble child He had softened her sufferings. For she looked round and asked dreamily how soon she and Felicitas were to be given to the wild cow, and when told that that part of their trial was over, she seemed to rejoice and gather new strength, though she could scarcely believe it. For it was the fearful thought of the wild beasts that had been the worst to her gentle spirit: death itself she did not fear. And it came soon, though to the last, all Perpetua's courage was called for. The gladiator who was to kill her trembled and shook; it is said he was unskillful — rather would one think he was conscience-stricken and filled with remorse. It was her own hand which guided the sword thrust to her tender throat. Her dear brother Saturus was already dead, though to the last, with holy unselfishness, he had encouraged and supported the others. That he would be the first to die had been foretold in one Perpetua's visions, in which she had seen a golden stair, up which Saturus ascended before her, ready to welcome her when she came. And so it was. In the vision Saturus heard his sister say, "Whatever happiness I have had in life is as nothing compared with what I have now." And the blessedness of heaven is no short-lived joy. "Eye hath not seen, nor ear heard, neither have entered into the heart of man, the things which God hath prepared for them that love Him."[23]

---

23   1 Corinthians 2:9

St. Christopher,
AD 249

Jetta Wolff

In old Gothic churches there is often seen among the carved stonework the figure of a man of great height, bearing upon his shoulders the infant savior: it is the statue of St. Christopher—the Christ-bearer. The story or legend of his life is very beautiful.

St. Christopher was at first a pagan, but he had always a good, kind heart, and as he was very big and strong—much bigger than most other men—he gave up his time to helping passengers across a ferry which was deep and dangerous.

One day as he lay asleep in his lodge by the river side, he thought he heard the voice of a child begging him to bear him across the stream. He rose at once, lifted the child upon his shoulder, and stepped into the river. But, lo, the water rose and swelled, becoming every moment higher and harder to pass through, while at the same time the child seemed to grow heavier and heavier, as St. Christopher went farther into the stream. The man stooped in pain under the weight, and he was full of fear lest both he and the child should be drowned. But he struggled on, and the other side was reached. Then the child told him He was Jesus Christ the King, and the next morning when Christopher arose, he found the staff he had leant upon as he passed through the waters had blossomed like a palm, and was covered with leaves, flowers, and fruit.

He prepared without delay for Baptism, became a sincere Christian, and before long gave up his life for his faith. This is the story. Much of it is what we call an allegory, that is, a story meant to show some great truth. The stream swollen and hard to pass through represents earthly life—life full of trial and temptation as it must always be for the earnest Christian. But bravely bearing Jesus in their hearts and his cross upon their shoulders, those who are faithful and strong reach at length the shores of heaven, there to reap the fruit of their good works, and to find that "inasmuch as ye have done it unto the least of these little ones, ye have done it unto Me."[24]

---

24   Matthew 25:40

St. Valentine, AD 270

Jetta Wolff

St. Valentine was so famous for his love and charity that the custom of choosing valentines upon his festival, which is still practiced, took its rise from him. The Church ordered that the 14th of February, till then a pagan holiday, should be observed by Christians in remembrance of the brave martyr. Perhaps it was the day of his birth, perhaps that of his death, we do not know. It may be that it was only a day near to one of these dates, which the people were accustomed to keep as a holiday, and which the Church was glad to dedicate to a Christian martyr, and forget that those around them kept it in honor of the idols they worshipped. The pagans, it is said, were used to write each other's names upon shells or small pieces of wood, and then to draw names to see who would be their partner for their dances on this day. The Christians, instead, in keeping their festival, wrote down the names of special saints and sent

words of loving Christian greeting to each other; and probably thinking of all the loving words and deeds of the martyred Priest, called their letters "valentines."

St. Valentine lived at Rome in the time of the Emperor Claudius II. He was a priest, and his life was one of constant self-devotion and Christian love. He spent all his time in doing deeds of mercy and charity, and in giving help and refuge to the poor persecuted followers of the faith of Jesus, for those were evil days for all Christian people.

The Emperor heard of him and commanded that Valentine should be brought into his presence.

"Why dost thou not worship as we do?" he asked. "Why dost thou refuse to bow before the gods of the Romans?"

The Christian priest looked calmly and without fear upon the emperor—upon the man who had power to condemn him to immediate death, to have him torn to pieces by the wild beasts or burnt to cinders at the stake. Unflinching, St. Valentine stood there before Claudius, and speaking out boldly and bravely gave reasons for his faith.

The emperor listened. He was struck by the priest's bold words, and by his clear reasoning. It was the story of St. Paul and Agrippa repeated: "Almost thou persuadest me to be a Christian."[25]

---

25 Acts 26:28

"Might not this Christian priest be right after all?" Claudius asked himself. "Was it not possible that what he and the Romans were used to call gods were indeed but low, vile creations of man?"

But he feared to say openly what he thought; only instead of ordering St. Valentine to be tortured or put to death, he gave him into the charge of a judge named Asterius, with whom he was to live, shut up, indeed, but not harshly treated.

Now the priest could no longer continue his works of mercy, but he could still pray. Day and night he entreated God for the poor Christians from whom he was parted, and also for the emperor and all those who were still in the darkness of heathenism, beseeching the Father that they might learn to know the True Light, Jesus Christ, His Son.

One day the judge Asterius heard him thus praying. "What is this thou sayest?" he asked. "What meanest thou by the words, 'Jesus Christ made Man,' and 'the True Light?'"

"I mean that Jesus, the Son of God the Father Almighty, became Man for our sake; and not only is He the True Light, but the only Light. He lighteth everyone that cometh into the world."

"I will test thy words," replied Asterius. "I have a little daughter who has been blind for two years. If by thy God thou canst make her darkness light and cure her blindness, I will at once believe that Jesus Christ is the Light of the World—that He Whom thou dost worship is God alone."

The legend tells us that God enabled Valentine to cure the young girl. He laid his hands on her and prayed and in a short time, we are told, the child had her sight restored, and saw clearly.

Then Asterius and his wife threw themselves, overjoyed, at the feet of the saint, and cried, "We believe, we believe! What must we do to be saved?"

St. Valentine told them to break in pieces the images of their false gods, to abstain for a time from worldly pleasures and rich living, to forgive all those they looked on as their enemies, and then to receive the Sacrament of Baptism.

Not only the father and mother of the maiden, but the whole household of Asterius followed the counsels of St. Valentine. They became known as a Christian family. Then they were called upon to suffer for their faith. Willingly they gave up their lives, as so many Christians had done before them. St. Valentine suffered, too, in a very short time.

Some years later, when the fierceness of persecution had ceased, and the "noble army of martyrs" in heaven were rejoicing over the comparative peace on earth, a church was built at Rome in remembrance of his good and holy Christian life.

St. George, AD 303

Jetta Wolff

St. George was born in Palestine of Christian parents. His father was an officer in the service of the Roman Emperor, Diocletian, and was rarely at home, so the boy was brought up chiefly by his mother. It was from her, no doubt, that he learned to be so gentle and kind and courteous, while at the same time he was always so brave and fearless. It is known that almost all our greatest men have had good mothers, whose counsels they have listened to, and whom they have loved to obey.

George was still young when his father died; following in his steps the boy became a soldier. He soon came to be looked upon as one of the bravest knights of the day, and he was made what is termed a "military tribune," and was thus placed in a position in the state which gave him some power in the government of his country. Then came a dreadful time of persecution for the Christians. It is known in history as the Diocletian persecution, as Diocletian was the emperor under whom it was carried on.

There is a story that the emperor was one day in a cave consulting the Roman god Apollo. The god, of course, did not really exist, but as the emperor stood before his statue, he believed not only that he was there listening to him, but that he was able to tell him what was likely to happen, and what he ought to do about peace and war, and other matters in the state. All this time a pagan priest stood by, inventing the answers supposed to be given by the god. Then the emperor thought he heard a voice from the cave, saying, "The just who are on the earth prevent me from telling the truth."

"Who are these just ones?" demanded the emperor.

"They are the Christians," was the answer.

Diocletian was enraged. He really believed it was the voice of a god, of a being who was all-powerful for good or evil, that spoke to him from the cave, and the idea that the Christians—"that new sect"—should stand in the way of his gods, was unbearable to him.

Now followed the terrible "Diocletian persecution." It was a fearful time. The Christians were hunted out of home and land, brought before the Roman judges, put to the most frightful tortures in the hope of leading them to give up their faith— beaten, burnt, put to death in the most horrible ways.

Then the knightly spirit of St. George was stirred within him. He took up the cause of the oppressed. Friends urged him to be prudent. "Your whole career is at stake," they said; "think a little of yourself, of your family; while you remain quiet, no harm will come to you. You are beloved by the emperor; he trusts you, and will overlook your own Christianity, but beware how you give help to others."

Their words were spoken in vain. St. George knew well his own danger. What was that to him while there were distressed men and women needing his aid, while there was cruelty and injustice going on which he might perchance help to redress[26]? Not only did the young man give all possible aid to those in trouble, he boldly went before the emperor and pleaded the cause of the Christians.

But Diocletian was stern and cold. "Young man, think of thine own future," was all he would say, and before St. George could reply, he was seized by a body of guards and carried off to prison. Then he, too, was tortured. They threw him roughly upon the bare stone floor, made his feet fast in the stocks[27], and laid a heavy stone upon his chest. He did not flinch, nor did he once waver either in his own faith, or in his will to help the persecuted, should he ever again have the chance. The next

---

26   To remedy or set right.

27   A device for punishing offenders made of a wooden frame where the feet can be locked.

day they stretched him on a wheel with sharp spokes, when it seemed to him as if he heard a voice from heaven, which said, "Fear nothing, I the Lord am with thee," and he thought he saw near him the form of a man clothed in white.

The emperor himself came to beg St. George to give way; he did not answer, but asked to be taken to the temple to see the gods Diocletian worshipped. The emperor thought the Christian knight was now at last overcome, and was about publicly to renounce his faith.

He gave orders that the Senate and all the people of Rome should come to the temple and be present at the great sacrifice which he believed St. George was about to make to the gods. Surrounded by his guards, the young man was led into the crowded building. All eyes fixed upon him, he went straight up to the figure of the god Apollo. He looked up at the image, beautiful indeed as a work of art, its lines all finely carved and molded, its substance of the rarest marble. But as his eyes rested upon the cold, hard limbs of the figure, the scorn of his soul gleamed from them, and through the vast building rang a loud, clear, startling voice, with the words, "Thou art not God!" The crowd of lookers-on seemed to surge like a great wave, and suddenly the idol was seen to totter on its pedestal, and fall to the ground, crumbling into a thousand pieces.

There was a cry that St. George was a magician, a wizard,

a man in league with the spirit of evil. The priests of the temple pressed the emperor to rid himself of the "Christian knight," and the next day, on the 23rd of April, A.D. 303, he was led out to meet his death.

There are many stories that have been told, stored up, and handed down from father to son, from one family to another, about that grand old knight. I will only tell you one here: the story of "St. George and the Dragon."

St. George was on his way to a certain city in Libya. As he journeyed, he came one day upon a maiden who was weeping bitterly, and slowly walking all alone towards the hills beyond the city gates. He stopped and asked her why she wept, and why she was thus alone without the city, for he saw at once that she was no common maiden, but a young girl of high rank.

Then she told him that there lived in the hills before them a strange and monstrous beast, which came down each day into their town seeking food. Full of fear, the people had given him sheep, two each day; but when after a while there were no more sheep left among them, they had been forced to give up their children, two at a time, to stay the hungry rage of the terrible creature, and save the lives of the rest of the people. Children under fifteen years of age, said the young girl, had been taken by lot, rich and poor alike, and at last the lot had fallen upon the only daughter of the king, that was herself.

At first, said she, her father would not give up his child, but the people were angry and mad with terror; they cried out that unless the king yielded his daughter, as they had given up so many of theirs, they would set fire to his palace and burn him and his family within it. He had been forced to give way, and she had come forth ready to die for her people; she had been put without the city walls, the town resounding with cries and groans as the great gates had closed upon her. Now she was walking towards her death—towards the cave of the fearful beast.

St. George listened horror-struck to the young girl's tale. When it was ended, he said quietly, "Fear not, I will deliver you."

The maiden could not believe this to be within his power, or the power of any man, and she urged him to leave her to her fate and save himself from danger.

"Fly, O noble youth! Tarry not, I pray thee. Fly, fly!" she cried.

But St. George had no thought of flying. "I will save you through the might of Jesus Christ," he said, firmly.

And then the dragon was seen slowly crawling out from its hiding-place in the hills and coming towards them.

"Fly, I beseech you! Fly, brave knight," cried the maid once more. "I am ready to die—leave me."

But the brave St. George bade the girl give him her sash, which was long and of fine strong silken cord, and then to stand back. Then he sprang upon the creature. There was a fierce struggle, but the knight mastered the beast, and bound him with the princess's sash.

He went into the city and showed the people what he had done. They fell on their knees before him; tears of joy streamed from the eyes of the women and children, while the men were ready to worship him as a god. The king clasped his rescued daughter to his heart and stood mute and breathless with emotion.

But the dragon was not yet dead, only tightly bound. St. George stood before the people and said, "It is through the grace and power of Almighty God, through the love of His Blessed Son Jesus Christ, the Savior of mankind, that I have been enabled to do this deed. Believe now in Christ and be baptized, and I will slay the monster before your eyes."

Twenty thousand people became Christians in one day. They felt that the faith which could give such power and courage, and such kindness of heart to the man who had saved them, must be of God, must come from the true Father and Creator. They felt that there was nothing in all their own vain religion to equal the love which had made the young man before them ready to sacrifice himself, if need be, for the good of a people all unknown to him. They felt that the strength by which he had overcome the beast was more than human, was given by a higher power. They bowed their heads and asked to be taught to know the God of St. George.

The king of the city offered the young knight great riches. He took what was given him, not for himself, but for the poor oppressed Christians of his own land. Nor would he stay at the court of the king, though much pressed to do so. He went forth on his way to Palestine. How he afterwards returned again to Rome, and there so nobly suffered martyrdom, you have already read.

St. Catharine of Alexandria, AD 305

Jetta Wolff

There were several brave Christian women who bore the name Catharine, and who in their lives and by their death showed themselves worthy to be counted among the saints of the Church. The Catharine I am going to tell you about was a princess of the ancient town Alexandria, at the mouth of the river Nile, in the north of Egypt.

If you have seen a firework's show, you may know what is called a "Catharine Wheel." It is one of the brightest and prettiest among the various pyrotechnics. You wouldn't have thought when you saw it flashing round that it gained its name from the wheel, surrounded by sharp spokes, which was invented to put a Christian woman to death. Hear the story.

Catharine was the daughter of a king. She was beautiful and clever, and very fond of study. Her father built her a high tower with rooms full of books and everything that was needed

for reading and for the study of the stars, a study in which she, like the philosophers of Egypt, took great delight. But when she was only fourteen years of age both her parents died, and she became queen over her father's lands.

Young as she was, Catharine was very wise. She governed well, but she liked to live simply and quietly, she hated pomp and show and fine dress, and all the state by which as a queen she was surrounded.

By-and-by it was thought right that she should marry. Catharine herself did not wish this. She was entreated to give way for the good of the state, and in order that there might be someone to lead out the armies in time of war. So she said if a very good and wise man could be found for her, then she would wed.

The night after she had given this answer to her ministers, she had a strange dream. She believed it was a vision. An old man seemed to come before her and give into her hands a picture of the Savior. Catharine was not yet a Christian, though she had learned the history of Jesus, and had dwelt much upon it. But from this night her faith, before uncertain, became firm and unwavering, and she did not rest till she had received the Sacrament of Baptism. At the same time, she said she could not now think of marriage.

It was no easy time at which to take up the Cross of Christ. The Emperor of Rome was hunting out and persecuting the

Christians wherever they were to be found, and the tyrant Maximin came to Egypt, laying waste the country and calling upon all men to make sacrifice to the pagan gods.

Taking her people under her protection, the young Queen Catharine went before the tyrant, and asked to be allowed to plead for her God and for the Christian Faith. A great meeting was called. The most learned men were bidden come together to discuss. The heathen priests and doctors were to speak for the gods they worshipped, Catharine to plead the cause of Christ the Lord.

By prayer and fasting she prepared herself for the trial day. When it came, she spoke so well that more than fifty men among the heathen there were overcome by her words and said they could no longer argue on the side of the Roman gods.

Maximin was furious. He ordered that everyone who would not bow to the gods he adored should be slain. Against St. Catharine he was especially enraged, for when he had first come into Egypt, struck by her great beauty, he had wished to make her his friend. But besides being a heathen and a tyrant, Maximin was in every way a bad, wicked man. When Catharine would have nothing to do with him, he tried all the means in his power to harm her, and now he thought of how he could most cruelly have her put to death.

So the dreadful wheel was invented—a great huge wheel

with sharp spokes all round, to which she was to be fastened, and then the wheel set in motion. But when everything was ready, and the cruel machine about to be turned, the cords broke.

The people cried out that the God of the Christians had worked a miracle to save His faithful servant. At this the agents of the emperor were only the more enraged, and by their order a soldier, quickly seizing a sword, cut off her head.

There are many beautiful old pictures of St. Catharine. Some of the most famous artists, touched by the beauty of her life, have made her the subject of their work. She is painted with a broken wheel near her, and sometimes also a sword.

St. Catharine was chosen in early times as the patron of Christian learning in schools.

ST. NICHOLAS OF MYRA, AD 343

JETTA WOLFF

There never lived a Christian bishop more honored and beloved than the good St. Nicholas; never one kinder of heart, or more helpful to all persons who were poor or in trouble. His parents had been very rich, and he was still quite a boy when both his father and mother died, leaving to him all their wealth. But even at that early age Nicholas was decided to "sell all he had and give to the poor."[28] He said he wanted little for his own life, and when, by-and-by, he became a priest, he would go about barefoot, sleep on a plank of wood for a bed, and neither eat meat nor drink wine. He said he was able to do without the good things of earth and was happy if he could save their cost in order to give the more to those that were in need. But in all that he did Nicholas showed himself to be wise as well as kind, and he would never give to mere

---

28   Matthew 19:21

beggars, or to people who were lazy and did not try to work. He would take great pains to find out who were in real want; then he gave all the help he could.

One day Nicholas heard of a man, once rich, who had lost all his money and fallen into great distress. This man had three daughters, all very beautiful. But they had never learnt to work, and now their poor father feared they would have to beg their bread in the streets, and he was quite heart broken.

One night it happened that the three girls were sleeping, and the poor father sitting near the open window of his house weeping bitter tears. Suddenly some gold coins were thrown in, some landing in the daughter's shoes. As soon as the father had overcome his surprise, he rushed out to see who could have done this. But there was no one anywhere to be found. The next night more gold coins were thrown through the window. The father heard no sound, and though he rushed out at once this time, he could see no one near. The third night the father sat again at his window; he had quite made up his mind that if more money were thrown in, he would find out who threw it. He strained his eyes through the darkness, and yes, in a little while there he saw a man coming on tip-toe under the shadow of the wall. He darted out and threw himself upon his knees before St. Nicholas.

When St. Nicholas had known of the poor man's trouble,

he had taken a sum of money and divided it into three portions, to be the dowry of the three daughters. He knew their father would put the money by and arrange it in such a way for his girls, as that they would each always have a little to live on and be spared the shame of beggary. But he was sorry to be found out in his good deed. He loved rather to "do his alms in secret"[29] and to be rewarded only "of His Father in heaven," not by the praise of men.

At one time St. Nicholas wished to go and live in a desert so as to be away from the world with its trials and temptations. But he had a dream in which he thought he heard a voice telling him to stay among the people and continue to do good in the world.

There are many stories of all he did. Once, we are told, he saved a number of little children from death in a time of war and famine, when a cruel innkeeper was about to slay them and offer their flesh as meat to the starving people.

At another time he was in a great storm on the sea. No one thought the ship could be saved. But St. Nicholas remained calm and fearless, and prayed earnestly to God. The wind went down; the sea grew quiet. Everyone said the calm was sent in reply to the prayers of the good Christian priest, and from that day he was looked upon as a patron saint of sailors.

---

29   Matthew 6:4

So through his whole life he went about doing good and helping others; and so he is said to come to you children at Christmas-time, and make you happy for that joyous season. For the Santa Claus who is supposed to steal down the chimney on the night of Jesus' birth and fill your stockings with just what you happen to want or like best, was once a real living man, who spent his life and wealth, not exactly in filling the stockings but in giving what they most needed to people in distress, and giving it whenever he could in secret.

"Santa" means saint, as no doubt you know; "Claus" is the short for Nicolaus, which is the German way of writing Nicholas. He conquered by his generous character.

The special friend of little children, of maidens in distress, of sailors tossing on the sea, the supposed donor of all our Christmas presents, good Santa Claus will live in our hearts and in the hearts of our children to all time, as, in his own day, he lived in the hearts of those who knew him or his good deeds. He will live to all time in the memory of man on earth below, to all eternity in heaven with the God he so faithfully served.

St. Antony the Great, AD 356

St. Athanasius of Alexandria

Selections from *The Life of St. Anthony* by St. Athanasius

Antony you must know was by descent an Egyptian:
his parents were of good family and possessed considerable
wealth, and as they were Christians he also was reared in the
same Faith. In infancy he was brought up with his parents,
knowing naught else but them and his home. But when he was
grown and arrived at boyhood, and was advancing in years, he
could not endure to learn letters, not caring to associate with
other boys; but all his desire was, as it is written of Jacob, to
live a plain man at home. With his parents he used to attend
the Lord's House, and neither as a child was he idle nor when
older did he despise them; but was both obedient to his father
and mother and attentive to what was read, keeping in his heart
what was profitable in what he heard. And though as a child
brought up in moderate affluence, he did not trouble his parents
for varied or luxurious fare, nor was this a source of pleasure

to him; but was content simply with what he found nor sought anything further.

After the death of his father and mother, he was left alone with one little sister: his age was about eighteen or twenty, and on him the care both of home and sister rested. Now it was not six months after the death of his parents, and going according to custom into the Lord's House, he communed with himself and reflected as he walked how the Apostles left all and followed the Savior; and how they in the Acts sold their possessions and brought and laid them at the Apostles' feet for distribution to the needy, and what and how great a hope was laid up for them in heaven. Pondering over these things he entered the church, and it happened the Gospel was being read, and he heard the Lord saying to the rich man, "If you would be perfect, go and sell that you have and give to the poor; and come follow Me and you shall have treasure in heaven."[30] Antony, as though God had put him in mind of the Saints, and the passage had been read on his account, went out immediately from the church and gave the possessions of his forefathers to the villagers — they were three hundred acres, productive and very fair — that they should be no more a hindrance upon himself and his sister. And all the rest that was movable he sold, and having got together much mon-

---

30   Matthew 19:21

ey he gave it to the poor, reserving a little, however, for his sister's sake.

And again as he went into the church, hearing the Lord say in the Gospel, "be not anxious for the morrow,"[31] he could stay no longer, but went out and gave those things also to the poor. Having committed his sister to known and faithful virgins, and put her into a convent to be brought up, he henceforth devoted himself to discipline, taking heed to himself and training himself with patience. For there were not yet so many monasteries in Egypt, and no monk at all knew of the distant desert; but all who wished to give heed to themselves practiced the discipline in solitude near their own village.

Now there was then in the next village an old man who had lived the life of a hermit from his youth. Antony, after he had seen this man, imitated him in piety. And at first he began to abide in places outside the village: then if he heard of a good man anywhere, like the prudent bee, he went forth and sought him, nor turned back to his own home until he had seen him; and he returned, having got from the good man (as it were) supplies for his journey in the way of virtue. So dwelling there at first, he confirmed his purpose not to return to the abode of his fathers nor to the remembrance of his kinsfolk; but to keep all his desire and energy for perfecting his discipline. He

31   Matthew 6:34

82

worked, however, with his hands, having heard, "he who is idle let him not eat,"[32] and part he spent on bread and part he gave to the needy. And he was constant in prayer, knowing that a man ought to pray in secret unceasingly. For he had given such heed to what was read that none of the things that were written fell from him to the ground, but he remembered all, and afterwards his memory served him for books.

Thus conducting himself, Antony was beloved by all. He subjected himself in sincerity to the good men whom he visited and learned thoroughly where each surpassed him in zeal and discipline. He observed the graciousness of one; the unceasing prayer of another; he took knowledge of another's freedom from anger and another's loving-kindness; he gave heed to one as he watched, to another as he studied; one he admired for his endurance, another for his fasting and sleeping on the ground; the meekness of one and the long-suffering of another he watched with care, while he took note of the piety towards Christ and the mutual love which animated all. Thus filled, he returned to his own place of discipline, and henceforth would strive to unite the qualities of each and was eager to show in himself the virtues of all. With others of the same age he had no rivalry; save this only, that he should not be second to them in higher things. And this he did so as to hurt the feelings of

---

32   2 Thessalonians 3:10

nobody, but made them rejoice over him. So all they of that village and the good men in whose intimacy he was, when they saw that he was a man of this sort, used to call him God-beloved. And some welcomed him as a son, others as a brother.

But the devil, who hates and envies what is good, could not endure to see such a resolution in a youth, but endeavored to carry out against him what he had been his custom to effect against others. First of all he tried to lead him away from the discipline, whispering to him the remembrance of his wealth, care for his sister, claims of kindred, love of money, love of glory, the various pleasures of the table and the other relaxations of life, and at last the difficulty of virtue and the labour of it; he suggested also the infirmity of the body and the length of the time. In a word he raised in his mind a great dust of debate, wishing to debar him from his settled purpose. But Antony, his mind filled with Christ and the nobility inspired by Him, and considering the spirituality of the soul, quenched the coal of the other's deceit. Again the enemy suggested the ease of pleasure. But he like a man filled with rage and grief turned his thoughts to the threatened fire and the gnawing worm, and setting these in array against his adversary, passed through the temptation unscathed. All this was a source of shame to his foe. For he, deeming himself like God, was now mocked by a young man; and he who boasted himself against flesh and blood was being put to flight by a man in the flesh. For the Lord was working with Antony — the Lord who for our sake took flesh and gave the body victory over the devil, so that all who truly fight can say, "not I but the grace of God which was with me."[33]

And the fame of Antony came even unto kings. For Constantine Augustus, and his sons Constantius and Constans the Augusti wrote letters to him, as to a father, and begged an answer from him. But he made nothing very much of the letters, nor did he rejoice at the messages, but was the same as he had been before the Emperors wrote to him. But when they brought him the letters he called the monks and said, "Do not be astonished if an emperor writes to us, for he is a man; but rather wonder that God wrote the Law for men and has spoken to us through His own Son." And so he was unwilling to receive the letters, saying that he did not know how to write an answer to such things. But being urged by the monks because the emperors were Christians, and lest they should take offense on the ground that they had been spurned, he consented that they should be read, and wrote an answer approving them because they worshipped Christ, and giving them counsel on things pertaining to salvation: "not to think much of the present, but rather to remember the judgment that is coming, and to know

---

33   1 Corinthians 15:10

that Christ alone was the true and Eternal King." He begged them to be merciful and to give heed to justice and the poor. And they having received the answer rejoiced. Thus he was dear to all, and all desired to consider him as a father.

And after many years he fell sick. Having summoned those who were there — they were two in number who had remained in the mountain fifteen years, practicing the discipline and attending on Antony on account of his age — he said to them, "I, as it is written (Joshua 23:14), go the way of the fathers, for I perceive that I am called by the Lord. And do you be watchful and destroy not your long discipline, but as though now making a beginning, zealously preserve your determination. For you know the treachery of the demons, how fierce they are, but how little power they have. Wherefore fear them not, but rather ever breathe Christ, and trust Him. Live as though dying daily. Give heed to yourselves and remember the admonition you have heard from me. Have no fellowship with the schismatics[34], nor any dealings at all with the heretical Arians[35]. For you know how I shunned them on account of their hostility to Christ, and the strange doctrines of their heresy. Therefore, be the more earnest always to be followers first of God and then of the Saints; that after death they also may receive you as well-

---

34 Those who divide the church.

35 See the next chapter for a discussion of the Arian schismatics.

known friends into the eternal habitations. Ponder over these things and think of them, and if you have any care for me and are mindful of me as of a father... And divide my garments. To Athanasius the bishop give one sheepskin and the garment whereon I am laid, which he himself gave me new, but which with me has grown old. To Serapion the bishop give the other sheepskin, and keep the hair garment yourselves. For the rest, fare ye well, my children, for Antony is departing, and is with you no more."

Having said this, when they had kissed him ... he died and was gathered to the fathers. And they afterward, according to his commandment, wrapped him up and buried him, hiding his body underground. And no one knows to this day where it was buried, save those two only. But each of those who received the sheepskin of the blessed Antony and the garment worn by him guards it as a precious treasure. For even to look on them is as it were to behold Antony; and he who is clothed in them seems to bear his admonitions with joy.

This is the end of Antony's life in the body and the above was the beginning of the discipline. Even if this account is small compared with his merit, still from this reflect how great Antony, the man of God, was. Who from his youth to so great an age preserved a uniform zeal for the discipline, and neither through old age was subdued by the desire of costly food, nor through the infirmity of his body changed the fashion of his clothing, nor washed even his feet with water, and yet remained entirely free from harm. For his eyes were undimmed and quite sound and he saw clearly; of his teeth he had not lost one, but they had become worn to the gums through the great age of the old man. He remained strong both in hands and feet; and while all men were using various foods, and washings and various garments, he appeared more cheerful and of greater strength. And the fact that his fame has been blazoned everywhere; that all regard him with wonder, and that those who have never seen him long for him, is clear proof of his virtue and God's love of his soul. For not from writings, nor from worldly wisdom, nor through any art, was Antony renowned, but solely from his piety towards God. That this was the gift of God no one will deny. For how did those in Spain and in Gaul, how in Rome and Africa, was the man heard of who abode hidden in a mountain, unless it was God who makes His own known everywhere. For even if they work secretly, even if they wish to remain in obscurity, yet the Lord shows them as lamps to lighten all, that those who hear may thus know that the precepts of God are able to make men prosper and thus be zealous in the path of virtue.

Read these words, therefore, to the rest of the brethren that they may learn what the life of monks ought to be; and may believe that our Lord and Savior Jesus Christ glorifies those who glorify Him: and leads those who serve Him unto the end, not only to the kingdom of heaven, but here also — even though they hide themselves and are desirous of withdrawing from the world — makes them illustrious and well known everywhere on account of their virtue and the help they render others. And if need be, read this among the heathen, that even in this way they may learn that our Lord Jesus Christ is not only God and the Son of God, but also that the Christians who truly serve Him and religiously believe in Him, prove, not only that the demons, whom the Greeks themselves think to be gods, are no gods, but also tread them under foot and put them to flight, as deceivers and corrupters of mankind, through Jesus Christ our Lord, to whom be glory for ever and ever. Amen.

Athanasius.

ST. ATHANASIUS OF ALEXANDRIA, AD 373

GEORGE HODGES

One day, in Alexandria, a bishop was standing by a window in his house, which looked out over the sea. He had invited some people to dinner, and they were late in coming, and he was waiting. When they came, they found the bishop so interested in what he saw out of the window that they looked also. On the shore of the sea a little group of boys were "playing church." One was the minister, the others were the congregation. The boy who was the minister called up the others one by one and baptized them in the sea; and this he did just as it was done in church, saying the right words and doing the right acts: The bishop beckoned to the boy. "What is your name?" he said. And the boy answered, "Athanasius."

Some years after, when Athanasius had come to the last year of school, the bishop took him into his own house, and he became his secretary, and the bishop loved him as a son. The lad desired to be a minister in earnest, and the bishop taught him, and at last ordained him.

Now the minister of the largest church in Alexandria was named Arius. He was a tall, pale man, careless in his dress, and with his hair tumbling about his head, but kind and pleasant to everybody whom he met, and a great preacher. His church was always crowded, and he was much admired for his goodness and his eloquence. But Arius and the bishop did not agree. And one time, in the presence of a large number of ministers, at a convention, Arius said aloud and publicly that the bishop was not a good teacher of religion. The bishop, he said, was seriously mistaken.

Alexandria, at that time, was much like Athens when it was visited by St. Paul. It was a place where the people loved to argue and debate. The Alexandrians were fond of discussing hard problems. They were, therefore, greatly interested in the debate between Arius and the bishop, and everybody took part in it, on one side or on the other.

Arius said to the bishop, "You teach that Christ is only another name for God, and that there is no difference. How can that be, when God is the Father and Christ is the Son? Is not the Son different from the Father? Is He not, indeed, inferior to the Father? There must have been a time in the far spaces of eternity when the Son began to be, when He was created like the rest of us. He is, of course, divine but in an inferior position." At this the bishop was filled with horror and declared that Arius was either making Christ a creature like man, or at least was robbing Him of so much of His greatness that He was not truly divine, or was setting such a difference between Him and God that there were two gods according to his teaching, two distinct gods.

This is not the place in which to discuss this difficult matter, as they discussed it in Alexandria. This much, however, may be said, that Arius in taking the names "Father" and "Son" literally, and making such inferences from them, was putting Christianity in danger of a pagan invasion. For if there may be two distinct gods, the Father and the Son, why not twenty, why not two hundred? We have to remember that a great part of all the people of Alexandria and everywhere else were pagans, and believed in many gods. Out of this the Christians had been saved. They had daily evidence of the confusion and doubt and evil living into which that belief brought men. Thus the doctrine of Arius, while to some it seemed reasonable enough, was really an attack upon the very central meaning of Christianity.

The emperor of the Roman world, at that moment, was a Christian. Constantine was the first Christian emperor. One day, as he was crossing the Alps at the head of an army, on his way to fight for the Roman throne which he presently won, he saw a bright light in the sky, like a blazing cross. And that night, in a dream, he saw Christ coming to him and telling him to go to battle with the cross upon his banner. Then when he was victorious and was made at last sole ruler of the world, he took the side of Christianity. He stopped the long series of bitter persecutions. He put an end to the effort which had been made by emperor after emperor to destroy the Church.

So when the debate which Arius began spread from Alexandria to other cities and threatened to divide the Christians into contending armies, Constantine interfered. One of his great hopes in siding with the Christians was thereby to bring about the unity of the people; and here were the Christians themselves divided. He determined to stop it by calling a great Christian council to decide the question.

The appointed place was Nicaea, near to where Constantine soon founded the city of Constantinople. To Nicaea, then, came bishops from all parts of the empire, from Carthage and Italy and Spain in the West, from India and Persia in the East. Some were lame and some were blind after the tortures of the persecutions. The president for the eastern churches was Eusebius of Nicomedia, the president for the western churches was Hosius of Cordova. All Christendom was represented. With the bishop of Alexandria came Athanasius.

The purpose of the council was to present to the world a statement of the true belief of Christians concerning the nature of Christ as found in the scriptures and Christian worship. This they did in terms which were afterwards used in what is called the Nicene Creed. Arius refused to sign it, and a few others agreed with him. They were expelled from the Church. Then the council was disbanded, and Constantine and everybody else thought that the trouble was happily ended. As a matter of fact, it was only begun.

No sooner had the bishops returned to their homes than the contention arose anew. Some liked the Nicene decision; others, as they considered it further, were not satisfied. And the unsatisfied ones were influential at the court. One was the chaplain of the emperor. Constantine was thus persuaded that Arius was right, after all. And what Constantine thought was the immediate opinion of many who knew little about it but were very anxious to stand well with Constantine. Against these Arians was Athanasius. Old Bishop Alexander had now died, and Athanasius had been made bishop in his place.

The dispute became a struggle between Alexandria and Constantinople, between Athanasius and Constantine. Arius himself presently died. He had been received by the emperor, and an order was issued that he should be restored to the communion of the Church. Arius was actually on his way to the service when he was seized with a bitter pain, so that he stopped in the street and sought refuge in the nearest house. The triumphal procession waited for him at the door. At last a man came out and said that Arius was dead. Constantine too came to the end of his great life, but his sons who succeeded him were on the Arian side.

Athanasius was banished from his city, and came back only to be banished again. Once on his return the rejoicings were so great that in after years, when the youth of Alexandria praised the splendor of any festival, the old men said, "Yes, but you should have been here on the day when Father Athanasius came home."

Troops were sent to Alexandria. Athanasius was besieged in the church where he was holding service. It was in the night, and the great church, crowded with worshipers, was dimly lighted with lamps. The soldiers broke down the doors, and with drawn swords made their way through the congregation, in the midst of wild disorder, to the chancel[36]. Athanasius was rescued by his friends after being nearly torn in pieces. He escaped to the desert.

One time he was pursued by his enemies on the Nile. As he rounded a bend of the river, in the dusk, he ordered his rowers to turn back. His pursuers came on with all haste and

---

36   Part of the church near the altar reserved for the clergy.

in the dusk of the late afternoon the two boats met. "Have you seen Athanasius?" the soldiers called across the water. "Yes," replied the bishop, "he is not far away!" Thus he escaped again.

This life of hardship and danger Athanasius lived because he was not willing to deny the true faith. The whole Church seemed to be against him. There was even a Latin phrase describing this time: Athanasius contra mundum – Athanasius against the world. Council after council was called by the emperors, attended by hundreds of bishops, making Arian creeds. The whole empire was thrown into confusion. Athanasius, on the other side, was preaching sermons and writing books and letters. The one man defied the Church. And he gained the victory! Year by year, it became plain that the theology of Arius was filled with confusion. People were perplexed by the long series of different Arian statements of belief. Athanasius maintained the divinity of Christ, in whom God dwelt among men. People were dismayed at the energy with which the Arian court used the swords of soldiers to maintain its side. The Church grew weary of the fierce debate. Then the last of the Arian emperors fell in battle with the Goths, and the war was ended. Theodosius, who succeeded him, was of the faith of Athanasius- the orthodox had prevailed.

98

St. Macrina the Younger and Her Family, AD 380

Sabine Barring-Gould

It is most rare to be able to obtain a glimpse into the home-
life of the ancients. In the first centuries of our era, in the Greek
and Roman world, life was so much in public that there was
hardly any domestic life at all; and it was only with Christianity
that the quiet, retired, and sweet home society constituted itself.

In the midst of flaunting paganism, the first believers were
driven indoors, so to speak; they were precluded from much
of the amusement that went to fill up the time of the heathen.
They could not sit on the benches of the amphitheater, nor
attend at the representations of the theatre. They were largely
prevented from being present at banquets given by friends,
as these began and ended with libations to the gods, and the
benediction of the deities called down on the meats. They were
precluded from taking part in civil life, by the oaths and sacrifices associated with every official act.

Thinking, feeling, believing differently from their fellow-citizens, they could not associate with them easily abroad, and were consequently driven to find their society in their own homes.

Perhaps it is only in the writings of St. Basil and his brother St. Gregory of Nyssa that we get anything like a look into the interior of a Christian household in the fourth century. It is therefore, although a quiet picture of an uneventful and unexciting existence, full of interest and charm. St. Basil belonged to a family both noble and wealthy, in Cappadocia, in Asia Minor. His ancestors had occupied public positions either as magistrates or at the imperial court.

His grandmother, Macrina, a native of Neocæsarea, in Pontus, had been brought up by St. Gregory the wonder-worker; and she and her husband, whose name is not recorded, were confessors in the persecution of Diocletian. They fled to the wooded mountain sides, leaving their houses and possessions; and in their places of retreat subsisted mainly on the wild deer, that were so tame that they allowed themselves to be easily snared. They remained in concealment for seven years, and it was not till an edict in favor of the Christians was promulgated, on April 30th, 311, that they ventured to return to Neocæsarea.

Macrina died in Pontus about 340. Her son Basil inherited the piety of his parents, and he took to wife Emilia, a woman of great virtue, the daughter of a man who had been put to death after having been deprived of his goods by the Emperor Licinius. She had lost her mother in early youth.

Basil and Emilia were very wealthy. They owned extensive estates in Pontus, Cappadocia and Lesser Armenia; they had a large family, ten children, of whom the eldest was Macrina, named after her grandmother; St. Basil was the eldest son, then came Naucratius, Gregory, afterwards of Nyssa, and Peter, the youngest, afterwards of Sebaste. We know no more of the four younger girls than that they were well provided for in marriage, and one of them had daughters who became superiors of a monastery in Cæsarea under the direction of their uncle, St. Basil.

Basil the elder, the father, died about 349, shortly after the birth of Peter. Emilia was now left a widow with a large family to look after, but she was assisted in everything by her eldest daughter, Macrina, who was her inseparable companion.

When Macrina had been born she had been confided to a nurse, but it was remarked that she was almost always in her mother's arms. Emilia took pains to form the mind of the little girl and give it a religious direction. She taught her first of all sentences from the Book of Wisdom, then made her commit sundry psalms to memory; so that, as her brother Gregory wrote, the Psalter became to her a companion day and night, and she was forever singing psalms or reciting them in her heart.

Macrina was a good and patient needlewoman. Not only was the house large, but the brothers and sisters needed attention, and their clothes keeping in order, and Emilia and her eldest daughter were constantly engaged at their needles, to keep pace with the demands of the family; and as they were always together, one mind was but the reflection of the other.

What tended to make Macrina a still, stay-at-home girl, was an early love affair. She had been engaged by her father's consent to a high-principled, well-born young man, and the marriage was only deferred because of Macrina's youth. But before this took place he fell ill of fever and was carried off rapidly. After this Basil thought of uniting his daughter to some other suitable person, but Macrina urgently entreated to be allowed to remain with her mother. "My dear husband," she said, "is not dead,—he lives with God. He has gone on a far journey— that is all, and I shall remain faithful to him whilst he is away."

Her father did not press her—indeed, the devotion of Macrina to her mother was so tender and so close that he thought neither could bear to be parted. When he also died, then the union of hearts and interests became closer.

As the children grew up, they dispersed and received their several inheritances; but they all carried away with them indelibly[37] the stamp impressed on their hearts by their mother and eldest sister; and in the end three of them became bishops and saints. Peter, the youngest, had been most in their hands, but the favorite brother was Naucratius.

As soon as all the birds were out of the nest, then Emilia felt that there was nothing to retain her in the city, and she pined to be away from its dusty streets and noisy market in the green, sweet country, and in quiet with God.

Accordingly, she and Macrina retired to a villa they possessed on the banks of the river Iris, at some little distance from the town of Ibora. This they converted into a sort of monastery. The slaves and other servants, if they chose to unite in the same life, were given freedom and accepted on the footing of sisters, no distinction being made between the members of the little community.

St. Gregory of Nyssa says of this society: "They were all as one in what they ate and drank, as to their furniture and cells[38], and there was no token that they belonged originally to different ranks in the world. There was no ruffle of temper among them, no petty jealousies, no suspicions, no spite .... all their occupation was in prayer and the singing of psalms, which went on night and day."

---

37   Permanently.

38   What we would call a bedroom.

Peter, the youngest, who had been ordained, lived near at hand. St. Basil also for a while lived in retirement not far off and was a help and comfort to them.

At length Emilia died, at an advanced age. None of her children were with her at the time except Macrina and Peter; however, as she was dying, the old and saintly woman murmured blessings on the absent darlings, and taking Peter by one hand and Macrina by the other, said, "Lord, I offer to Thee my first fruits and my tithe. Accept them, O Lord, and pour the floods of Thy grace into both their hearts." They were her last words. She died in 373 and was laid beside her husband whom she had loved so well. The grief of Macrina was not to be expressed. She had been the inseparable companion of her mother since her earliest infancy, and they had not had a thought or wish but what was in common.

Before Macrina had recovered from this blow she was called on to endure another. Her favorite brother, Naucratius, was found dead in the field along with his servant Chrysapius, without it being known what had caused their death.

Six years later she was called to mourn the loss of her eldest brother, St. Basil. It was she who, with his friend Gregory Nazianzen, had been the means of turning his heart entirely to God. As a young man he had been disposed to push his way as a statesman. In 355 Basil had been at school with Julian, afterwards Emperor, and an apostate from the faith, and with Gregory, who was the son of the Bishop of Nazianzus. Basil had not formed a high opinion of the former, but with Gregory "it was one soul in two bodies." On returning to Caesarea after his father's death, Basil turned towards a life in the world, and a prospect of advancement in official life opened to him. It was then that Macrina had exerted all her influence over him and gave him that final direction which made of him so glorious a saint and teacher of the Church.

And now Macrina had lost him.

In the month of September or October in the year following the death of St. Basil, Gregory—now Bishop of Nyssa— was present at the Council held at Antioch, and on leaving it he resolved on paying a visit to Macrina. He had not seen her since the death of their brother Basil, and he wished to talk with her about him. The journey was long, and the snows were already powdering the lower ranges of the lofty mountains he had to pass.

On the night previous to his arrival on the banks of the Iris, after a tedious and long day's travel, he had a dream. It seemed to him that he held relics in his hands that emitted a blaze of white light.

When he awoke he wondered what this dream could signify; but as he neared the monastery he met a servant who told him that Macrina was dangerously ill, and Gregory at once concluded that his dream was a portent[39] of her approaching death.

Sick at heart, he pressed forward, and arrived at the villa. Those within came forth to welcome him, except the sisters, who remained in the church, sorrowful at the prospect of losing their best friend, yet glad that she should see her brother before her death.

Gregory at once entered the church and prayed and gave his benediction[40] to all. Then he asked to be conducted to Macrina.

We have an account of the last scene from his own pen, and this shall be given with only a little condensation.

"A woman who was there opened the door to me and led me within. I found my sister lying on the ground, on a plank covered with sackcloth (the Cilician material made of goat's hair, much in use for blankets) and with a pillow of the same supporting her head. She was very ill, but when she saw me, unable on account of her great weakness to rise and meet me, she lifted herself on one elbow, placing the other hand on the ground for her support. I ran to her and insisted on laying her down again as she had been. Then she lifted her hands to Heaven and said, 'I thank

---

39   A sign of something important.
40   A formal blessing.

Thee, O Lord my God, in that Thou hast fulfilled the desire of my heart.'

"She did her utmost to conceal from us what a difficulty she found in breathing, so as not to increase our distress; and her face was bright and smiling, and she spoke of such matters as she thought pleasing to us. But when we came to mention Basil, then my face expressed the grief I was in at his loss. But she, on the contrary, spoke of the matter with serenity of soul and elevation of mind, so that I felt myself as though carried up above all worldly considerations into heavenly regions with her.

"Presently she said, 'Brother, you have had a tedious journey, and must be very tired: I pray you take a little rest.' And although it was a delight to me to listen to her, yet I obeyed; and I went forth into the garden, where was a pleasant shady walk. However, I was in such trouble of mind that I could admire nothing, and I could think only of what must shortly happen.

"I suppose she must have divined my thoughts, for she sent word to me not to fret, as she hoped speedily to be better; but she really meant that she would escape from her present pains, and be with God, for whom her soul ever thirsted. I got up when I heard this and went to see her again. Then, when we were together, she began to talk about old times, since our childhood, and all as calmly and consequently as though she were reading out of a book. She talked of the mercies shown by God to our father, mother, and all the family.

"I wanted to tell her about my troubles when the Emperor Valens banished me for the Faith, and of other troubles in which I had been involved; but she cut me short with 'Never lose sight of the obligations you owe to God. Think chiefly of the advantages you have received from Him.'

"As she was speaking, we heard the song of the virgins calling to vespers[41], and my sister bade me go to the church. Thus passed the night, and when day dawned I could see clearly by her condition that it would be her last, for the fever had exhausted her last powers.

"My soul was agitated by double feelings: one was grief, for nature would make me feel, and I knew that the words I heard were the last that would be uttered by one very dear to me; the other was admiration at the calm and trust with which she awaited death.

"The sun was nigh setting without her having lost the force of her mind. Then she ceased to speak to us, but folded her hands and fixed her eyes on her heavenly Bridegroom. Her little bed was turned with the feet to the east, and she spoke to Him in a low voice, which we could hardly hear. We did, how-

---

41   The service of evening prayers.

ever, collect some of her words: 'O Lord, Thou deliverest us from the fear of death; Thou makest the close of life the commencement of a new and truer life. Thou sufferest us to sleep awhile, and then wilt call us with the trumpet at the end of time. To the earth Thou entrustest the dust of which Thy hands have fashioned us, to reclaim it and clothe it with immortality and glory. Lord, Thou who on the Cross didst pardon the malefactor, remember me in Thy kingdom.'

"Then Macrina made the sign of the cross on her eyes, her mouth, and her heart; and, the strength of the fever having parched her tongue, we could no longer follow her, but saw that her lips continued to move. She closed her eyes; but when a lamp was brought into the room she opened them, and made a sign that she desired to recite vespers. But her tongue failed her, only her spirit was active, and her lips and hands moved as before, and we understood when she had finished, by her again signing herself.

"Finally, she drew a long, deep sigh, and passed away in prayer. Seeing what had taken place, and remembering a wish she had expressed to me, in our last conversation, that I should render her the last offices, I put out my shaking hand to her face to close the eyes and mouth. But I did this only to fulfil my promise, for really there was no need, as eyes and mouth were closed, so that she appeared rather to be sleeping than dead. Her hands lay on her breast, and her body rested modestly, as that of a virgin."

When Macrina was being prepared for burial, there was no other raiment of hers found save her veil, her mantle, habit, and a pair of worn-out shoes. Then Gregory gave one of his own tunics for clothing his sister's body, and over her was cast her mother's black cloak; "and," says Gregory, "the blackness of this cloak made her face seem so much the whiter, as though it shone with light."

As she was being clothed, a widow, who loved her and attended to these last offices, untied a slender string that was round her neck, and released a little cross and an iron ring.

"Keep the cross," said Gregory to the widow, "as a remembrance of her; and I shall ever preserve the ring."

Who can tell? Perhaps that poor little iron ring was the reminiscence of her engagement to the young man to whom she had long ago been betrothed, and to whom she had remained ever faithful.

It is interesting to think that this faithful and pious woman had been the teacher of two of the greatest theologians the church has produced: her younger brothers, St. Basil the Great and St. Gregory of Nyssa.

St. Ambrose of Milan, AD 397 (& St. Augustine, AD 430)

Jetta Wolff

St. Ambrose was the youngest of the three children of Ambrosius, Prefect[42] of Treves under the Gauls. Theirs was a Christian family, and from the days of their earliest childhood till parted by death, the two brothers and the sister remained tenderly attached to each other.

It happened one summer day that the little child Ambrose was lying asleep in his cot in the court of his father's palace, when a swarm of bees came towards him, settled on the face of the ruddy baby boy, and flew in and out of the child's open mouth. The nurse in a panic of fear was about to make war upon the bees, but just at that moment the father, mother, and little ten year old sister came by.

"Do not touch them!" cried the father. He knew, no doubt, that if the bees were made angry, they would be sure to sting

---

42   A regional governor.

St. AMBROSE.

the child very badly. Also there was a common notion that the swarming of bees in a house or on a person was a good omen. Anxiously the parents stood by the cradle of their still sleeping boy, but the father forbade any movement that might disturb the swarm. Very soon the bees flew up high in the air, so that they were no longer to be seen; the child was unhurt, and the father said, "My boy will be something great."

The little Marcellina heard the words, and they took deep root in her young sisterly heart. Their father died while the children were still young, and we read of Marcellina helping her mother in the care of her little brothers, who were both some years younger than she was; and as Ambrose grew up, she never ceased to hold before him the high ideal she had formed of what he should one day become. Later the young girl took the veil as a Sister of Mercy, devoting herself to acts of charity in the service of God; but for some years all four, the two brothers, Marcellina, and their mother, lived together at Rome, where they went after the father's death, and where the boys carried on their studies.

They were a happy and united Christian family. Ambrose always looked up to Marcellina, and called her his "holy, venerable sister." At Rome they met with people of all kinds. The city was still in great part pagan; temples for the worship of the gods were on every side, and among their friends the family of

St. Ambrose counted many who were not Christians. But they kept firm in their own faith, and they were always held in high esteem in Rome and throughout all Italy.

By-and-by an office under government was given to Ambrose. The emperors lived at Milan at this time, and their affairs of State were carried on there; so quite early in his life Ambrose was sent to that city, which to this day honors him as the patron saint of the town and of all the nearby country. In the grand old city itself and in the little villages for miles round, St. Ambrose of Milan is spoken of with pride— "Our St. Ambrose."

"Go," said the Prefect Probus, who sent him thither, "and act not merely as an officer of the law, but as a bishop." By this he meant that Ambrose was to have a fatherly care for the city, to be wise and kind as well as just; but the words "as a bishop" were to come true to their very letter.

There were great disputes going on in Milan at this time. The bishop of the city, who had been a bad man, and had held wrong ideas about the Godhead of Christ, had just died. A meeting was called to elect a new one. In the nave of the old cathedral, or basilica as it was then called, were the people; a curtain separated them from the clergy in the choir. Affairs were in disorder, and the people in an uproar. Ambrose went into the building and began to speak to the crowd.

There was a moment's silence as the words of the young stranger fell upon their ears. In the midst of the lull the voice of a child was heard crying, "Ambrose is bishop! Ambrose is bishop!" The young prefect drew back. He had not yet even received the Sacrament of Baptism, for it was the custom in his day, in many Christian families, that baptism should take place after long preparation at a mature age. But the people had taken up the cry. As they looked upon the noble form of the young man, and heard his clear frank voice, it seemed to them that no better person could be found to govern them and their Church, for the bishop at this time had much to do with the ordinary affairs of the city. Surely, they thought, the voice of the child was the voice of God directing their choice. So, after much resistance, he was forced at last to yield. In a few days he was baptized. Then a week later he was ordained priest, and consecrated bishop.

With earnestness and faith he gave himself up to the work of his new and sacred office. His brother Satyrus went to join him at Milan and was of great help to him. His sister, the devoted Marcellina, also came at times, nursed him when he was sick, and set in order the affairs of his household. When not together the brothers and sister wrote to each other, and their letters remain to this day a record of pure devoted lives and true family affection.

But soon a great grief came to them. Their brother Satyrus was shipwrecked in a journey to Africa. He threw himself into the sea and swam to shore, but an illness followed from which he did not recover. For a few days St. Ambrose was prostrate with sorrow, but he roused himself to preach at the funeral, and the sermon still exists.

So devoted and noble was the daily life of the saint, so full of power his preaching, that he gained unusual influence over the rest of the clergy, and indeed over all men. Everywhere he was looked up to as a great leader: it was said to be his voice that guided the whole of Italy in the right way. He lived through the reigns of four Emperors of Rome, and it can never be known how great was the power for good which St. Ambrose, in his wisdom, had over them. It was a power which made itself the more felt because the saint was always so personally humble and simple, while at the same time so brave and fearless when he saw rebuke needful. Never would he give consent to a deed that he thought wrong or unjust, however urgently a king or Emperor might press it on him, however great his own danger in refusing to bend to the will of those in power.

He had many troubles. Once he was in great peril of losing his life. There were tumults in Milan. Justina, the widow of the Emperor Valentinian I, was what is termed an Arian—that is, one who denies that Jesus Christ as the Son of the Father is Himself really God. It was on account of this heresy in the Church that the Nicene Creed was drawn up, in which, you know, we say clearly, we believe Jesus to be "true God from true God, begotten, not made; of the same essence as the Father." Justina wished to turn one of the chief Christian churches in the city into a temple for her own way of worship. Her son, Valentinian II, took her part.

St. Ambrose strove indeed to teach Christians to be just to all who did not think as they did, but give up the House of God for false worship, that he would never do.

It was in the Lent[43] of the year 385. On Palm Sunday, just as St. Ambrose had ended his sermon and was about to celebrate the Holy Eucharist, news was brought him that agents of the emperor were storming the church for the Arians. A few moments later he was told that an Arian priest had been taken prisoner.

"Molest no one," was his order. "Touch no man; only guard the sacred building." And he at once sent some of his clergy to set free the captive.

Then came officers of Valentinian demanding whether he would not now give up the church.

"Never!" was his reply. "Take all I have, though indeed I

---

43   The time of preparation and fasting before Easter.

have nothing; my goods are only in keeping for the use of the poor. But take all, rob God's poor if you will, and take my life. I am ready to give it to save the altar of the Lord."

Holy Week was truly a time of suffering for the faithful Bishop. But the citizens of Milan were devoted to him. They did not wish to use arms against the emperor, but never would they desert their bishop. They went in bands, some to protect the church against the Arians, some to listen to the preaching of St. Ambrose, and to defend him if attacked.

Valentinian, who was not bad at heart, saw that he would do well to yield, and before Easter Day he withdrew the order he had given to take the Christian church.

It was indeed with joy that the Feast of Easter was kept in the city of Milan in the year of our Lord 385.

But the young emperor could not repress a feeling of jealousy at the love shown by the people to St. Ambrose, and at their courage in his behalf.

"You would give me up bound hand and foot to your bishop if he but said the word!" he cried in anger. Then one of the chief officers of the state, wishing to gain favor in the eyes of his master, swore he would take the life of the saint. He gave secret orders for his murder, and it is said that one night an assassin made his way to the bed where St. Ambrose lay sleeping, but that at the moment when he was about to raise his hand, it fell useless, stricken by the terrible malady of paralysis.

The next year the Arians tried again to get the church for their temple. The bishop was threatened with exile; but again the people of Milan kept true to him, and he was protected against his foes. Then the emperor gave way entirely, and himself came under the influence of the saint.

It was at this time that St. Augustine of Hippo was turned to Christ. The story of his conversion is very striking.

Augustine was a highly educated young Roman, clever, excitable, and quick-spirited. He had been brought up as a Christian, though not baptized; but on going to college he had let himself be led away from all the good he had been taught at home, and for some years he lived a very wild, evil life. Augustine had a mother named Monica; she was a good and holy Christian woman, and she ceased not day and night to pray for her son, whom she loved very dearly. He had come to live at Milan, and here he met St. Ambrose. Augustine was so struck by the life and bearing of the saint that, unbeliever though he was, he would often go to hear him preach, and he loved nothing better than to take every chance of talking with the bishop. But still he kept his evil way of life and his unbelief.

When Monica saw the respect which her son felt for St. Ambrose, she went one day and begged to speak with him. As she was led into his room, the mother, overcome by her feelings, burst into tears. Then, weeping still, she spoke and implored the bishop to talk to her son, and urge him by every means in his power to change his life and become a Christian.

Ambrose did not say much in reply; he had already marked the young man, he had also taken note of his character, and he knew that if he were to gain over him the power the mother wished, he must work very slowly and gently, and must not be hasty in urging him to take up the cross. So he would not promise what Monica asked, but only bade her be patient.

At this the poor mother's tears flowed afresh. She told St. Ambrose how she ceased not to pray for her son; "and now, my lord, I beg but this one thing—hear the pleadings of a mother, and speak to my child." Still all the bishop could say was, "Patience!"

Weeping, Monica turned away. Then Ambrose called her back. "Be comforted," he said, "the child of those tears can never perish."

And now in the spring of the year 386 the mother's tears were changed into smiles of eternal thankfulness. It was during the few days that the bishop, guarded by his faithful flock, was kept shut up in his basilica at the second attempt to set up Arian worship in the city, that St. Augustine was fully gained to the faith of Christ. St. Ambrose spent the time in teaching and preaching, and Augustine was among the throng that listened.

The services he held were bright, for the bishop was very musical, and he taught the people to sing psalms and hymns. He also composed many beautiful prayers for them, which remain to this day.

And now the soul of Augustine was touched and overcome. He felt that the God of St. Ambrose was God indeed, and he begged for baptism. It is believed that our glorious psalm of praise, the Te Deum, was composed by Ambrose and Augustine when the baptism took place.

Augustine soon afterwards went to Africa, and he became one of the grandest and noblest saints and bishops of the Church in after days.

One can picture the joy of St. Monica now. She did not live long after this. But she died truly, entirely happy. Her eyes had seen the salvation of the Lord, and her heart over-flowed with thanksgiving.

St. Ambrose was now left at peace. Theodosius became Emperor and was much attached to him, but the bishop was as firm with him as with others when there was a question of right and wrong.

Once, after a riot was stirred against him, Theodosius had caused numbers of the people to be put to death without even staying to see who among them were guilty, who innocent. Then, with the soldiers of his guard, he appeared before the basilica, thinking to give thanks to God for his victory over the rebels. But St. Ambrose met him at the door and forbade him to enter. Firmly and plainly the bishop spoke, showing the emperor how wrong he had been, and bidding him return and repent of his hastiness, and make amends to the living for the dreadful slaughter of the dead. "First be reconciled to thy brother, then come and offer thy gifts."[44]

Theodosius listened, till, sorry and ashamed, he turned from the House of God to come back as a penitent—that is, one who goes openly to church to beg forgiveness for a particular sin.

Justly proud may be the city of Milan to have had such a bishop, and proud his country of an emperor who humbly bore the rebuke of the Priest of God, and in the eyes of his people confessed, saying, "I have done wrong."

The beautiful old Church of St. Ambrogio stands to remind us of this noble saint. Few travelers pass through Milan without visiting it. Every corner tells us something of the work, the life, the teaching of him whose name it bears. And in the center of the choir, beneath the high altar is his tomb, where lights are still always kept burning.

He died in the year 397. He was not yet fifty years of age, but his strength was worn out. He had seen trouble in the church in his day, but it was a time of peace and quiet for the

---

44   Matthew 5:24

Christians when the faithful servant was called to keep his Eastertide in heaven. His arms crossed upon his breast, his lips moving in prayer, he passed from earth.

"Lord now lettest Thou Thy servant depart in peace, for mine eyes have seen Thy salvation."[45]

---

45   Luke 2:29-30

ὁ Ἅ Ἰῶ   ὁ Χρυσό
ᾳ   τό
               μο

St. John Chrysostom, AD 407

George Hodges

The name Chrysostom means golden-mouth, and it was given to a man in Antioch whose other name was John. He had prepared himself for the work of the ministry by years of privation[46] and solitude in the mountains, thinking and praying and listening to the voice of God in his soul. When he came out, he had a burning message to men about their sins. And he feared no living man. He was poor, and preferred to be poor. He asked nothing, except an opportunity to speak. And when he spoke, it was with an eloquence which made his hearers cry or laugh or tremble, as he pleased.

Thus Chrysostom ministered to Antioch. He preached daily. He taught to people the uncertainty of all the riches and pleasures of this life and urged them day by day to store their treasures in heaven, and to lay hold upon that happiness which

---

46   Lacking adequate food and warmth.

no chance or change can spoil.

When the bishop of Constantinople lay dead, and the churchmen were eagerly discussing who should sit in his great seat, secret messengers of the emperor were sent to Antioch, and they stole Chrysostom. They asked him to get into their carriage, and when he was once in, away they drove, at post haste[47], much against his will, to Constantinople, and there he was made bishop. The bishop of Alexandria, who was much disgusted, having other plans, was forced to consecrate him.

Thus Chrysostom became bishop of Constantinople, and found himself in the midst of the imperial court.

The first thing which he did was to take all the fine furniture which had belonged to his rich and luxurious predecessor, and put it out in the street, and sold it at auction. He dismissed all the servants. The splendid dinners, for which the bishop's house had been famous, came to a sudden end. The new bishop was as poor as the poorest of his people. All the money which came to him he spent for the relief of the needy and the care of the sick.

Then he preached, as he had done at Antioch, terribly plain sermons about sin; and not about sin in general, but about the actual temptations and sins of the people to whom he spoke. He reproved them for the ways in which they made their money,

---

47   Latin phrase meaning at great speed.

and for the ways in which they spent it. He reproached them for the cries and groans of their slaves, which he heard from their windows as he passed by in the street. He even criticized the clothes of the ladies. He spared nobody, the court least of all. The proud, luxurious, and selfish life of the emperor and the empress and their friends he disliked exceedingly, and said so plainly.

From the people, he proceeded to speak his mind about the clergy. He found them idle and neglectful of their duties, and called them to account. Some he reproved, some he expelled. Thus every day, by every word he said, he made an enemy. They were enemies of the right kind, who had no place in the friendly approval of a true bishop, but they were many, and some of them were in places of great power. They were able, and more than willing, to do him harm.

Thus the ministry of Chrysostom in Constantinople was very hard. He was as eloquent as ever, and the churches were crowded to hear him.

Now, the empress Eudoxia had caused to be erected, in the square fronting the cathedral, a statue of herself. It was of silver, on a porphyry column. And on the day when it was set up there was such a clamor outside the church, with dancing and singing, that Chrysostom could scarcely hear himself preach. He expressed his displeasure in his blunt manner and his words were reported to the empress. It was the crisis of a long hatred. The anger of the court caused the clergy to be angry as well. They were all against the righteous bishop, all whose evil lives he had condemned. The bishop of Alexandria had left his own city to trouble Chrysostom. Councils had convened to find some fault in him, like the councils which made false charges against Athanasius. The affair of the silver statue brought the full storm upon his head. Arcadius, whose father, Theodosius, had trembled before Ambrose, ordered Chrysostom into exile. And he had no powerful friends to help him in such a struggle.

Out he went, then, into exile. And as he went, a black smoke began to rise from the city, and flames beneath the smoke. The cathedral was mysteriously on fire. It was destroyed; and the great houses of government around it joined in its ruins. And beneath the charred and broken beams and stones which filled the square, lay the porphyry pedestal and the silver statue of Eudoxia.

They carried the old man, under a guard of soldiers, the whole length of Asia Minor, from Constantinople at the northwestern corner to the region above Antioch, in the southeastern corner. It was much the same journey which Bishop Flavian had made when he went to intercede for Antioch with Theodosius. But his place of exile was too near his friends to please his enemies. Letters of sympathy came to him by every mail, from the bishop of Rome, from the bishop of Milan, from bishops of the East who braved the enmity of the court. And every mail carried back letters from Chrysostom to his faithful people in Constantinople, who were suffering for his sake, to bishops and churches asking for his counsel. He speaks of exile and famine, war and pestilence, siege and solitude, as belonging now to his daily life. The place of his exile was bitterly cold in winter, and there were brigands who came down from the mountains to steal and kill. But he kept his courage and his good cheer.

At last an imperial order directed that he should be carried north to the shore of the Black Sea. Chrysostom was ill, and the summer was hot; the journey was long and difficult. The guards who conducted him had been given to understand that if their prisoner should chance to die by the way, it would be to their advantage, they would be paid so much the more. And die, he did. Beside a village in Pontus he sank down and could go no further. They dragged him on, but he was evidently dying. They took him to a little chapel, and there, crying, with his last breath, "Glory be to God for all things!" he passed away.

The life of Chrysostom differed from the life of Ambrose as defeat differs from victory, but the two men were intent on the same thing. The emphasis of the ministry of Athanasius was upon the creed: he magnified the importance of the creed. But the emphasis of the ministry of Ambrose and of Chrysostom was upon the essential and pre-eminent importance of character. That, they said, is the very heart and life of the Christian religion.

St. Patrick of Ireland, AD 461

Jetta Wolff

Most of you have heard of St. Patrick. I dare say you know also that he is called the "Patron Saint" of Ireland—that St. Patrick's Day is a great feast day for all Irish people wherever they may be.

But there are many people who know just as much as this, and not a word more about St. Patrick, save perhaps the old legend which says that he sent away from his country for ever all the creatures we call reptiles, that is, those which crept along the ground like snakes and adders. So they have learnt to think of this saint as a sort of wizard, or one who used magic arts, or even to believe that such a man never really lived at all.

But St. Patrick did live and was indeed a great and good man. It is a grand thing that the land he lived and worked in so many hundred years ago should still so greatly honor him.

Patricius, from which the name Patrick comes, meant a

Roman of noble birth. All Britain was under Roman rule at the time of St. Patrick's birth; and Roman families had come and settled in the land, just as in later times the Normans came with William the Conqueror. We cannot be quite sure in what part of Britain St. Patrick was born. We know that his father held office under the state, and there is a good deal of reason to think that his birthplace was Dumbarton in Scotland, and that there he grew up till he was about sixteen years old.

As a boy he was like most other boys of his age, very fond of play, and loving above all things to have his own way. From some writings of his which have come down to us, it seems as if he were even rather a naughty boy—that he cared little to please his masters. But when he was sixteen a dreadful thing happened. A band of robbers (or pirates, as they were called) fell upon the place where Patrick lived. They wounded his father, carried off his sister and sold her to be a slave, and took Patrick and a number of other boys and men, put them on board ship, and sailed with them across the sea to the coast on the other side, which was the county of Antrim in Ireland. Here Patrick was sold to be a slave to a rich man named Milchu and set to tend cattle on the hills. During six long years he spent most of his time alone among the woods and fields. He thought over his past life and felt that he had done much that was wrong—that he had cared little to do what was right, or to serve God or man through his early years. He believed God had let him be carried away from his home and sold as a slave because he had been so idle and careless, and that he might be led to a better life. He turned to God in earnest prayer. Out upon the hills in time of frost and snow, heat and cold—alone amid the thick woods and the green slopes beneath the clear bright sky, he gave up his whole soul to his Father in heaven. And by-and-by he felt that the Holy Spirit of God came and dwelt in his heart and made him burn with the wish to lead a good and noble life. Then one night he heard in a dream a voice saying to him, "Thy fasting is well; thou shalt soon return to thine own land."

His heart was full of hope and gladness, but he could only go on quietly with his work of tending the cattle, till after a little time he again had a dream. He thought he heard the same voice, and that it told him the ship was ready to take him away, but that it was two hundred miles off. At once he left the cattle and fled towards the seacoast. He reached it, found indeed a ship, and got over to France.

How great must have been Patrick's joy to find himself a free man after all those years. And not only did he find himself free, but in the midst of his own friends. For his parents had settled in France, and they were indeed happy to see back once more their long-lost son. But the heart that had been so truly drawn to God could not now rest content with a life of ease.

Once more St. Patrick had a dream. He saw in the midst of the night a man who came from Ireland, whose name was Victor. He had many letters, one of which he gave to the saint. It began: "The voice of the Irish;" and as he read aloud, he thought he heard the voice of those who were near the wood of Tochlut, which is near the Western Sea, crying out, "We entreat the holy youth to come and walk still among us."

So about the year A.D. 432 St. Patrick took a few men, and sailed across to Ireland. He landed first at the mouth of a river just where the town of Wicklow now stands. But he did not stay there: he wanted to go to the part where he had been kept so long captive, to teach the people there the good news of Jesus Christ.

He went on round the coast till he came to Strangford Lough. Here, he and his men left their boats and set out to explore the land. Before they had gone far, they met a swineherd, who thought this band of strangers must surely be pirates; so he ran off fast to call his master, a great Irish chief named Dichu, the son of a king.

Dichu came out sword in hand. But he was so struck by the calm and holy face of St. Patrick that he laid down his sword, took him to his house, and showed him great kindness. By-and-by Dichu became a believer in Jesus Christ—the first person in Ireland whom St. Patrick led to the Savior. He was very earnest, too, in his faith. He gave over to St. Patrick a piece of ground to build a church, which was called Sabhall Padbrig, meaning Patrick's barn. Very likely a barn had stood before where St. Patrick now built his church. Or perhaps it was called St. Patrick's barn because, as it was the first church he built in Ireland, it was very simple and plain, and, like all the early churches of those days, had a flat square roof and no tower.

St. Patrick would not stay very long as he wished so much to get on to the place where he had passed those six years of his life as a slave. So he gave Dichu his boats to take care of, and went on to Dalaradia, in Antrim, now known as "The Route."

When Milchu, who had been Patrick's master, heard of his coming he was full of fear. He could not think that a man whom he had owned as a slave could have become powerful except by magic arts, and thought he in his turn would be made a slave by the man whom he had used hardly in past days. But he said to himself that this should never be. So he piled up in his house all his goods and his riches, and placed himself on the top of the great heap he had made. Then he set fire to the house, and thus was burnt to death, he and all he had.

How great must have been the horror of St. Patrick as he drew near to this burning mass!

He set out next day for a place called the Hill of Tara, where lived most of the great lords and chiefs of Ireland. It was a grand old place. Ruins of its fine halls are still to be seen, and also great mounds beneath which many of the Irish kings and chiefs of those days were buried.

Before St. Patrick had got quite as far as the Hill of Tara he made a halt. It was just Eastertide, and he wanted to keep this great feast as fitly as he could. So he set up his tent on the Hill of Slane, a little way from the Hill of Tara, and on Easter Eve he made what in those old days was known as the "Easter fire." This was done by setting light to a number of tapers and candles, which made a great blaze that shone out through the dark night, till it was almost as bright as day.

But just at this very time the Irish king at Tara was keeping one of his pagan feasts. He had made it a law that no light or fire was to be seen anywhere over the whole land before the beacon-light shone out from his palace. By this law anyone who made a light or fire before that of the king was seen must be put to death.

And now, behold, the king and all the princes and nobles at Tara saw the great blaze of St. Patrick's blessed Easter fire.

The king in a rage called his chief Druids[48] to him and asked them the meaning of the light he saw.

---

48   A leader of the ancient Celtic religion (a form of paganism).

Then the Druids cried, "O king, live forever! This fire which has been lighted before the royal fire will never be put out if it be not put out this night. It will conquer our fires, and he who has lit it will conquer us all."

The king in great anger took some of his chief men and went out at once to attack St. Patrick. As they drew near one of the king's wise men begged him not to go too close to the Christian fires lest they might have some strange power over him. So he sent for St. Patrick to come out to him, and gave command that none of his people should rise as he drew near.

When the saint saw the king and his horses and cars he began to sing in the words of the psalm, "Some put their trust in horses and some in chariots, but we trust in the Name of the Lord our God."[49]

No one rose as he approached except a lad named Eric, one of the king's pages. He became a Christian later, was ordained priest, and was made in after-years Bishop of Slane—of that very part where he had thus first seen St. Patrick, and where, in spite of the king's order, he had risen to greet him. A small chapel, called after his name, still stands on the spot on the banks of the river Boyne.

One of the Druids who was with the king began to blaspheme—that is, to use impious words, and take the Name

---

49   Psalm 20:7

of the Lord God in vain. In an instant he was struck down dead. Then the king ordered St. Patrick to be seized, but at that moment a strange darkness came over the land, and there was a great earthquake. The guards fled in fear, and the king and queen were left alone with the saint. The queen went up to him and begged him not to slay the king. The king himself also bent low, and said he was ready to worship St. Patrick's God. He did not really mean this, and from the moment he felt free from danger he again tried to kill St. Patrick. But this he could not do. Then, after some time, he asked to be baptized, and he gave St. Patrick royal leave to pass on through Ireland. The king was never really a Christian. Fear alone, and the wish of the great lords of his court had led him to accept baptism. He died a pagan at heart. But after a time, many of his relations learnt from St. Patrick to believe in the Savior.

Let me tell you a beautiful story of two young girls whom he met and taught to know Jesus Christ.

In his travels he came once to a wide plain, where stood a palace and a sort of Druid college, in which young girls were brought up and taught. The king about whom you have just heard so much had sent his two daughters here. They were both very handsome; the one was called Ethne the Fair, the other Feidelen the Ruddy.

The two girls used to rise very early in the morning and go out to bathe in a well which was near the palace. One morning, what was their surprise to find close to this well a number of grave priests sitting with books in their hands.

The maidens said to them, "Who are ye, and whence do ye come?"

St. Patrick said, "It were better for you to learn to know the true God than to ask about our race."

Then one of the maidens asked, "Who is God, and where is God?"

So St. Patrick began to teach them, and they believed with all their hearts. But they wished to see the face of Christ. St. Patrick told them that it was only through death that they could come to see the face of the Savior. Yet they desired much to see Christ. Then they received from St. Patrick the Sacrament of Holy Communion, and a very little while afterwards they died, both about the same time, in the freshness of their youth and of their faith.

On the spot where their bodies were laid, close to the well, St. Patrick built a church.

In the course of his life, Patrick preached and taught through the whole of Ireland.

When at last he felt that he had grown old, and knew that he soon would die, he made his way back to the place where he had done his first Christian work. The monks, who had all loved him so dearly, could not agree as to where he was to be laid in his last long rest. The men of Armagh wished to have him in their midst; the men of Down wanted to keep him near them. At last they said they would settle the dispute by a sign. So the monks of Saul took two oxen which had never been tamed, yoked them to the cart which bore the body of their beloved master, left them quite without guide, and watched to see which way they would turn. The oxen went on till they came to that spot where stands now the Cathedral of Downpatrick. There they stopped and stood still.

It is believed that the bones of St. Patrick still lie beneath this cathedral.

St. Bridget of Kildare, AD 525

Amy Steedman

The mist of long years enfolds the story of Bridget, the dearly loved saint of Ireland. Though we strive to see her clearly, the mist closes round and only lifts to show us, here and there, a flash of light upon her life, and while we gaze in wonder the light is gone.

But all the time, behind the mist, we feel there is a gracious presence, a white-robed maiden with a pure strong soul, who dwelt in the green isle of Erin[50]; a gentle saint who dwells there still in the hearts of her people to bless and comfort them as of old. The mist of years cannot dim the eyes of those who love Saint Bridget's memory, nor can it bewilder their faithful hearts. Wise men may dispute the facts of her life, but to the poor, who love her, she is just their friend, the dear Saint Bridget whose touch made sick folk well, whose

---

50 The Irish word meaning "Ireland."

blessing increased the store of the poor, who helped sad weary mothers, and bent in loving tenderness over many a tiny cradle in those long-ago days.

In the first days of early spring her little flame-spiked flowers speak to them from the roadside, and bring her message of joy and hope, telling of the return of life, the swelling of green buds, the magic of the spring. We call her flower the common dandelion, but to Saint Bridget's friends it is "the little flame of God" or "the flower of Saint Bride." She herself has many names. Bride or Bridget, "Christ's Foster-Mother," Saint Bridget of the Mantle, the Pearl of Ireland.

Many stories and legends have grown up around the memory of Saint Bridget, but all agree in telling us that she was a little maiden of noble birth, and that her father, Dubtach, was of royal descent. We know too that she was born in the little village of Fochard in the north of Ireland, about the time when good Saint Patrick was beginning to teach the Irish people how to serve the Lord Christ.

Bridget was a strange and thoughtful child, fond of learning, but clever with her hands as well as her head. In those days even noble maidens had plenty of hard work to do, and Bridget was never idle. In the early morning there were the cows to drive out to pasture, when the dew hung dainty jewels upon each blade of grass and turned the spiders' webs into a miracle of flimsy lace. The great mild-eyed cows had to be carefully herded as they wandered up the green hillside, for, should any stray too far afield, there was ever the chance of a lurking robber ready to seize his chance. Then, when the cows were safely driven home again, there was the milking to be done and the butter to be churned.

But in spite of all this work, Bridget found time for other things as well. There was always time to notice the hungry look in a beggar's face as she passed him on the road, time to stop and give him her share of milk and home-made bread, time to help anyone in pain who chanced to come her way. The very touch of the child's kind, strong little hands seemed to give relief and many a poor sufferer blessed her as she passed, and talked of white-robed angels they had seen walking by her side, guiding and teaching her. And sure it was that in all that land there was no child with so kind a heart as little Bridget's, and no one with as fair a face.

Now the older Bridget grew the more and more beautiful she became, and her loveliness was good to look upon. She was as straight and fair as a young larch tree; her hair was yellow as the golden corn, and her eyes as deep and blue as the mountain lakes. Many noble lords sought to marry her, but Bridget loved none of them. There was but one Lord of her life, and she had made up her mind to serve Him.

"We will have no more of this," said her father angrily; "choose a prince of noble blood, and wed him as I bid thee."

"I have chosen the noblest Prince of all," said Bridget steadfastly, "and He is the Lord Christ."

"Thou shalt do as thou art bidden and marry the first man who asks thee," said her brothers, growing more and more angry.

But Bridget knew that God would help her and she prayed earnestly to Him. Then in His goodness God took away her beauty from her for a while, and men, seeing she was no longer fair to look upon, left her in peace.

At this time Bridget was but a young maiden of sixteen years, but old enough, she thought, to give up her life to the service of God. The good Bishop Maccail, to whom she went, was perplexed as he looked at the young maid and her companions. Did she know what God's service meant, he wondered? Was she ready to endure hardness instead of enjoying a soft life of pleasure and ease?

But even as he doubted, the legend says, he saw a strange and wonderful light begin to shine around the maiden's head, rising upwards in a column of flame, and growing brighter and brighter until it was lost in the glory of the shining sky.

"Truly this is a miracle," said the bishop, shading his eyes, which were blinded by the dazzling light. "He who, each morning, sendeth His bright beams aslant the earth to wake our sleeping eyes, hath in like manner sent this wondrous light to clear my inward vision and show my doubting heart that the maiden is one whom God hath chosen to do His work."

Even then the careful bishop sought to know more of Bridget's life ere he trusted the truth of the miracle. But there was nought to tell that was not good and beautiful. Out on the green hills, at work in the home, all her duties had been well and carefully performed. Happy, willing service had she given to all who needed her help, and there was but one fault to be found with her.

"She gives away everything that comes to her hand," said her parents. "No matter how little milk the cows are giving, the first beggar who asks for a drink has his cup filled. If there is but one loaf of bread in the house, it is given away. The poor have but to ask, and Bridget will give all that she can find."

"That is true," said Bridget gently, "but ye would not have me send them hungry away? Is it not Christ Himself we help when we help His poor?"

"Well, well, perhaps thou art right," answered her parents; "and this we must say, that in spite of all that is given away, we have never wanted aught ourselves, but rather our store has been increased."

Hearing all this, the bishop hesitated no longer, but laid his hands in blessing upon Bridget's head, and consecrated both her and her companions to the service of God. And it is said that as she knelt before the altar, while the bishop placed a white veil upon her head, she leaned her hand upon the altar step, and at her touch the dry wood became green and living once more, so pure and holy was the hand that touched it. At first there were but few maidens who joined themselves with Bridget in her work, but as time went on the little company grew larger and larger. Then Bridget determined to build their home beneath the shelter of an old oak tree which grew near her native village. It was from this oak tree that the convent[51] was known in after years as "the cell of the oak" or Kil-dare. Here the poor and those in distress found their way from all parts, and never was any poor soul turned away without help from the good sisters and the tender-hearted Bridget. Here the sick were healed, the sorrowful comforted, and the hungry fed. Here the people learned to know the love of Christ through the tender compassion of His servant.

Far and near the fame of Bridget spread, not only in Ireland but over many lands, and the love of her became so deeply rooted in the hearts of the people, that even to-day her memory

---

51   A Christian community of nuns or monks who have taken monastic vows.

is like a green tree bearing living leaves of faith and affection.

There are so many wonderful stories clustering round the name of Saint Bridget that they almost make her seem a dim and shadowy person, but there is one thing that shines through even the wildest legend. The tender heart and the helping hand of good Saint Bridget are the keynote of all the wonders that have been woven around her name. We see her swift on all errands of mercy, eager to help the helpless, ready to aid all who were oppressed, and protecting all who were too weak to help themselves.

One story tells us of a poor wood-cutter who by mistake had slain a tame wolf, the King's favorite pet, and who, for this, was condemned to die. As soon as the news was brought to Saint Bridget, she lost not a moment, but set out in the old convent cart to plead with the King for his life. Perhaps her pleading might have been in vain had it not been that as she drove through the wood a wolf sprang out of the undergrowth and leapt into the wagon. Loving all animals, tame or wild, Saint Bridget nodded a welcome to her visitor and patted his head, and he, quite contentedly, crouched down at her feet, as tame as any dog.

Arrived at the palace, Saint Bridget demanded to see the king, and with the wolf meekly following, was led into his presence.

"I have brought thee another tame wolf," said Saint Bridget, "and bid thee pardon that poor soul, who did thee a mischief unknowingly."

So the matter was settled to every one's satisfaction. The king was delighted with his new pet, the poor man was pardoned, and Saint Bridget went home rejoicing.

Those sisters who dwelt in the Cell of the Oak seemed to be specially protected from all harm, and it is said that many a robber knew to his cost how useless it was to try and rob Saint Bridget.

Once there came a band of thieves who, with great cunning, managed to drive off all the cows belonging to the convent, and in the twilight to escape unnoticed. So far all went well, and the robbers laughed to think how clever they had been. But when they reached the river which they were obliged to cross, they found the waters had risen so high that it was almost impossible to drive the cows across. Thinking to keep their clothes dry, they took them off and bound them in bundles to the horns of the cows, and then prepared to cross the ford. But Saint Bridget's wise cows knew a better way than that, and immediately there was a stampede, and they set off home at a gallop, and never stopped until they reached the convent stable. The thieves raced after them with all their might, but could not overtake them, and so, crestfallen and ashamed, they had at last to beg for pardon and pray that their clothes might be returned to them.

In those days there were many lepers in Ireland, and when there was no one else to help and pity them, the poor outcasts were always sure of a kindly welcome from the gracious lady of Kildare. One of the stories tells of a wretched leper who came to Saint Bridget, so poor and dirty and diseased that no one would come near him. But like our blessed Lord, Saint Bridget felt only compassion for him, and with her own hands washed his feet and bathed his poor aching head. Then, seeing that his clothes must be washed, she bade one of the sisters standing by to wrap her white mantle round the man until his own clothes should be ready. But the sister shuddered and turned away; she could not bear to think of her cloak being wrapped around the miserable leper. Quick to mark disobedience and unkindness, a stern look came into Saint Bridget's blue eyes as she put her own cloak over the shivering form.

"I leave thy punishment in God's hands," she said quietly; and even as she spoke, the sister was stricken with the terrible disease, and as the cloak touched the beggar, he was healed of his leprosy.

Tears of repentance streamed down the poor sister's face, and her punishment was more than tender-hearted Saint Bridget could bear to see. Together they prayed to God for pardon, and at Saint Bridget's touch the leprosy was healed.

So Saint Bridget lived her life of mercy and loving-kindness, and because the people loved and honored her above all saints, they placed her in their hearts next to the Madonna[52] herself, and, by some curious instinct of tender love and worship, there came to be woven about her a legend which has earned for her the titles of "Christ's Foster-Mother" and "Saint Bridget of the Mantle."

It was on that night, so the legend runs, when the Blessed Virgin came to Bethlehem, weary and travel-worn, and could find no room in the village inn, that Saint Bridget was sent by God to help and comfort her. In the quiet hours of the starry night, when on the distant hills the wondering shepherds heard the angels' song, Saint Bridget passed the stable door and paused, marveling at the light that shone with such dazzling brilliance from within. Surely no stable lantern could shed such a glow as that which shone around the manger there. Softly Saint Bridget entered and found the fair young mother bending over the tiny newborn child, wrapping His tender little limbs about with swaddling bands.

There was no need to ask who He was. Bridget knew it was the King, and kneeling there, she worshipped too. Then very

---

52   From the Italian "madonna" or "my lady" which came to mean the Virgin Mary.

tenderly she led the young mother to a soft bed of sweet hay and prayed her that she would rest awhile.

"Sweet Mary," she implored, "rest, and I meanwhile will watch and tend the child." And Mary, looking into Bridget's kind blue eyes, and feeling the touch of her tender strong hands, trusted her with her Treasure, and bade her take the child and watch Him until the morning should break.

So Bridget took off her soft mantle and wrapped the baby in it, and, sitting there, rocked Him to sleep, crooning to Him all the sweetest baby songs she knew.

Perhaps it was Saint Bridget's tender love for little children, and her gentle care for all poor mothers, that helped to weave this curious legend, but there is a beautiful truth hidden deep in the heart of the strange story too. For did not Christ Himself say of all kind deeds done to the poor, "Inasmuch as ye have done it unto one of the least of these my brethren, ye have done it unto Me"[53]; and again, "Whosoever shall do the will of My Father which is in heaven, the same is My brother and sister and mother."[54]

So it is that Saint Bridget bears the name of Christ's foster-mother and is linked in this loving way with the Mother of our Lord. Year by year her memory lives on, and when Febru-

---

53   Matthew 25:40
54   Matthew 12:50

ary, the month of Saint Bride, comes round, when the bleating of the first lambs is heard on the hills, and the little flower of Saint Bridget lights up the wayside with its tiny yellow flame, the thought of good Saint Bridget, Christ's foster-mother, fills many a poor mother's heart with comfort. Did she not care for all young things and helpless weary souls? Did she not show how, by helping others, she helped the dear Lord Himself? Does she not still point out the way by which they too may find Him and live in the light of His love?

St. Benedict of Nursia, AD 543

Jetta Wolff

St. Benedict was born in Noricum, in the country of Nursia in Italy. He was of good family, and at the age of seven the boy was sent to Rome, under the care of an old and faithful nurse, to be educated.

The city at this time was very carefree and very sinful; it was given up wholly to selfish pleasures, and somehow or other the young Benedict came to see a great deal of the evil that was going on. He was filled with horror, and at last, when he was about fourteen, feeling he must see no more of such wickedness, he left Rome and fled to a lonely place among the Sabine Hills.

Here he met a monk, by name Romanus. To him the lad poured out his heart. The monk spoke kind words of counsel, gave him a hair-shirt and a goat-skin cloak, and advised him to remain for a time among the hills away from men. So Bene-

Schraudolph pinx. 382. Adr. Schleich sc.
Einsiedeln (Switzerland) Benziger Brothers, Publishers.

St. Benedict.
He was filled with the Spirit of righteousness.
(St. Gregory.)

dict buried himself in a deep hollow between high rocks, from whence he could see nothing but the blue sky above. His food was a small portion from Romanus' own fare, thrown down to him at the end of a rope with a bell tied to it, which Benedict rang each time he wanted the rope pulled up. In this strange way the young man passed three years. Thorns and thick bushes grew around his hiding place. Now and then he would come up from his hollow, and walk about among the bushes, but all this time he saw no one save the monk Romanus or the poor peasants of the country near. The peasants thought at first that the being whose home was the hidden rock, his food the rudest herbs, his way of life so singular, must be some strange wild animal, half man, half beast. But soon they saw that he was indeed a man like themselves, and that he had moreover a good kind human heart. They learned to love him first for the kind words he spoke whenever they met, and by-and-by for his good deeds and his teaching. For as St. Benedict felt himself growing stronger and more fit to contend with the evil of the world, he came out more often and began to teach others and to make himself known as a servant of God.

By-and-by some monks asked him to go and be at the head of their convent. But they soon found him too strict. St. Benedict in his mountain solitude had made himself able to bear what they were either unwilling or unable to endure. There must have been some very bad men among them, for one day they gave him a cup of poison. Perhaps the saint knew of their bad designs. At any rate he did not drink of the cup, but making the sign of the cross, shivered it into a thousand pieces. Then he left this monastery.

But men who, like St. Benedict, had felt the evil of the world too overpowering, or its temptations too strong for them, and who, longing to live a holy life, sought solitude, gathered round him, and he founded a number of monasteries, placing in each twelve monks. So he tried to help others and to serve God. But troubles and temptations still followed him, and at last he said he must travel away by himself and live quite alone for a time. He went along by the Apennine Mountains till he came to the hilly spot called Monte Cassino. Here he settled down, teaching, preaching, training himself, and working among the people for fourteen years; and here, upon the site of an ancient pagan temple, he built his famous monastery. The sick, the poor, the sinful, all came to Father Benedict. He was never harsh or severe in his dealings with the weak and fallen. By all he had gone through himself, he had learned how to treat with gentleness and wisdom the failings of his fellowmen. The Order he formed is kept up still and is still full of life. The original monastery of Monte Cassino has long since passed away, the building now standing on the same spot being of much later date; but the Order of St. Benedict has lasted through more than 1,500 years. The rules he drew up and followed, the dress he arranged, are still kept to.

Once a fierce Gothic chief, named Zalla, who had plundered a great many poor Italian peasants near Monte Cassino, caught one of them and put him to cruel torture, trying to force him to give up the little he had to live on.

The peasant would not yield to the brigand chief, and at last he cried out that he had nothing left of his own, that he had given all to the Abbot Benedict.

Zalla at once bound the poor man's arms behind him, and rode up the steep hill of Monte Cassino, driving the peasant on before him, as if he were an ox or a mule. They found the Abbot reading before the gate of his monastery.

"There is the Father Benedict of whom I told thee," cried the peasant.

"Rise, rise!" cried the fierce chief from his horse. "Rise, I say!" he cried to the Abbot.

St. Benedict looked up calmly. He did not move from his seat, nor did he seem in the least disturbed. But he said quietly, "Give back what thou hast taken from this poor man." As he spoke, he looked at the poor bound peasant till it seemed as if his cords loosened of themselves; and the angry Goth, cowed by the quiet sternness of the saint, fell from his horse, trembling and overcome, at the Abbot's feet.

Benedict took him into the convent, set the best of their simple food before him, and then, in burning words of indignation, spoke to him of his cruelty and injustice. The peasant left the place a free man.

St. Benedict had a sister to whom he was greatly attached. She, too, had given herself up to serve God as a "religious," and lived at a convent that was not very far from Monte Cassino. But he did not think it right for him to visit his dear sister often, so they used to arrange a meeting once every year; and as the day came round, Scholastica, as she was called, would go out of her own gate to meet her brother on the mountainside. The last time they were thus together, Scholastica was feeling far from well. Her health was failing; she knew she was going to fall ill. But she would not say much about herself to her brother, only when evening came and it was time for St. Benedict to depart, she said: "My brother, leave me not tonight."

"What is this thou sayest, my sister?" he exclaimed. "At no cost can I stay a night out of my monastery."

Scholastica bent her head, clasped her hands upon the table, and wept silently.

Suddenly there fell upon their ears the sound of rain and storm. The weather till then had been calm and bright. In a moment all had changed. The sister looked up with a gleam of joy. Benedict could not leave his shelter that night. "God is hearing me!" she cried. "Brother, I prayed to thee, thou wouldst not listen. Then I prayed to God, He is hearing me."

They parted in the morning to meet no more on earth.

St. Benedict had the body of his sister taken to Monte Cassino and laid in the tomb he had ready for himself. He lived but forty days longer. A fever attacked him. He felt that he was about to die. After six days of suffering, he begged to be carried to the chapel. Then he bade his monks open the tomb where his sister had been laid six weeks before. He went up to it, stretched out his arms to heaven, and so stood in prayer. And then, standing thus, he died—a soldier's death—struggling to the last moment against the weakness of mortal nature. He had fought "manfully all his days against the world, the flesh, and the devil;" he had continued "Christ's faithful soldier and servant until his life's end." Then—

The golden evening brightened in the west,
To him, the faithful warrior, came the rest,
Sweet is the calm of Paradise the bless'd, Alleluia!"[55]

---

55   From the hymn "For all the Saints" by William Walsham How.

St. Columba of Iona, AD 597

Jetta Wolff

St. Columba was an Irishman—Irish by birth, descent, and education. His native place was Gartan, a wild part of Donegal, where the great clan to which he belonged still exists. His family was of high rank, closely related to one of the Irish royal families of those days. You will not forget his name when I tell you that it means a dove. It is a Latin name, and from it has come the French word for a dove, columbe.

Christianity had already been taken to Ireland; there had been Roman Priests, teachers, and scholars in the island for two or three hundred years before St. Columba's birth, so it is not strange to find many of the educated Irish bearing Roman names.

Columba was a man of great learning. From boyhood he had loved work, and at the large college or school for monks at Clonard where he was brought up, he studied under great men, and worked very hard. Very hard he worked all his life long—first as a young student, then as a priest, and later as a bishop. St. Columba was always busy. Studying, teaching, preaching, or writing, his was an activity that never flagged.

He was one of the greatest scribes or writers of the day. Printing had not yet been invented, many of the "books" of those early times, and indeed of much later ones, were rolls of parchment, a very strong kind of paper made from the skins of sheep and goats. Upon this, men copied out by hand the holy Gospels, the books of prayer, the writings of the Fathers, besides works of history, medicine, science, and whatever else they had of literature in those days.

This copying was one of the chief occupations of every monastery, and not only time but a great deal of care was given to such work, especially to all the sacred writings. They were copied out in beautiful colored letters, and were done so well that even to this day the colors remain bright and unfaded. You may see many of these old "books" in the great libraries, and among the belongings of the old cathedrals and churches.

One day a friend lent St. Columba a fine manuscript of the Psalms, which he cared for so much that he thought he would make a copy for himself just like it. But when the friend saw this copy made by St. Columba, he said that as it was written from his book it must belong to him. This seemed to St.

Columba very unjust, and he refused to give up what he had written out. Then the friend was very angry, and had the matter tried before the king of the county. It seems very strange to us, but the king said St. Columba was in the wrong, and that the copy he had written belonged by right to the owner of the manuscript he had made it from.

It was now Columba's turn to be angry. He called all his friends to him, and there was a great fight between the counties of Ulster, where lived Columba, and Meath, the land of the king who had judged against him. The party of Columba won, and many of the Meath men were slain.

But to be thus the cause of a great fight was a terrible sin in a man who was a Priest of God, and when it was over Columba himself was the first to see how wrong he had been, and to submit to punishment. He was ordered to leave his own land, his home, and all that he loved, and to go to the country of the Picts—Pictland, as Scotland was then termed—there to spend his life in trying to turn the people to Christianity.

So he sailed away with twelve monks, and landed first at a small island. He set himself to explore the land, and climbed to the top of one of the hills. From this point he saw, far, far away, the cliffs of his own country. Tears must have filled his eyes at that sight, for he had been ordered never to look on Ireland again. And as he gazed now, he thought, "No; it cannot be right for me to stay here, where I may look any day upon my beloved land. I must sail farther."

He took to his boat again, and went on till he came to Iona, from which no trace of Ireland could be seen.

Here he worked with vigor for many years. He first set himself to learn the language of the Picts. He had with him two priests who were Picts by birth, and with them he studied till he was quite able to speak and teach the people in their own tongue. There was a prince reigning in the country named Brude; he was very strong and powerful. Columba thought how great a thing it would be for the land and the people, if the king could be won to Christ. It was a bold act for the poor stranger Christian Priest to go to the palace of the great prince, but Columba did not hesitate. He went to Brude, and soon both the king and many of the great lords of his court received the Sacrament of Baptism.

The Druids tried hard to upset his work; many were the trials and troubles he was called on to endure, but he struggled on valiantly through them all, and in the end, he gained great power in the land. Everywhere he founded monasteries and churches.

Then after many years he went back to his beloved Ireland, but not for his own pleasure. A decree had been sent out by the Parliament of the country—in those days only an assembly of great chiefs—that the bards must be banished from the land. These bards were minstrels or poets who went about from one great castle to another, singing and reciting their poems. The country was in a disturbed state. Instead of one king over the whole land, there were a number of petty rulers in the different parts of the island, and it was feared the bards, by singing first in honor of one, then of another of these wild chiefs, helped to stir up strife and discontent among their people. But when St. Columba heard of this decree it seemed to him to be very unjust, and he at once went before the assembly of chiefs and so well urged the cause of the poor minstrels that the law against them was put aside, and they were allowed to remain in their land. The bards were very grateful to the saint, and the chief among them, the poet laureate of the island, wrote a poem in his honor.

He stayed some time in Ireland, but when he felt old age upon him, he went back to Iona, there to pass his last days. After four years the end came. It was Saturday morning. The old saint rose as usual, and went out into the fields to see the monks at their labor, and to bless them in their work. Then he visited the barn, where was stored the grain and hay. All was in order, there was provender[56] enough to last till the next harvest

---

56   Dry food for domesticated animals such as hay or oats.

time. He turned homewards. When about halfway he met the old horse which for years past had day by day carried the milk from the dairy to the monastery. The animal came up and laid his head on the master's shoulder, as if to take leave. There was a sad look in the eyes of the aged beast, as if he knew the parting was at hand.

The monks who were with him would have driven away the animal, but St. Columba forbade them. "The horse loves me," he said, "leave him alone, leave him with me; let the poor beast weep for my departure; the Creator has revealed to this poor beast what is hidden from man," and he spread out his hands and blessed the dumb animal.

He went on home, and, entering his cell, sat down to work at a copy of the psalms. When he came to Psalm xxxiv. II, he laid aside his pen. "I must stop here," he said, "Bathene will finish the rest."

He then sent a last message to his disciples and followers, begging them to live always in peace and charity. This was the 9th of June, 597.

When the midnight bell rang for the Matins[57] of Sunday, St. Columba rose from His couch, and ran to church before the other monks. Hastily the attendants followed him. They found him lying before the altar. He opened his eyes, and turned them

---

57   The service of morning prayers.

upon his brethren, with a look of serene and holy joy. He raised his right hand to bless; then he passed away, his face calm and sweet like one who in his sleep had seen a vision of heaven.

Magnum Gregorium,
quem procumbentem ante Deiparæ imaginem, adverso in pariete depictam
cuius ipse dum viveret alloquium meruit,
Annibal Caraccius, urgente Salviatæ Gentis pietate, coloribus expresserat,
Ex archetypo à se delineatum æri incidit, ut omnium voto faceret satis
Iacobus Frey.

ST. GREGORY THE GREAT, AD 604

JETTA WOLFF

Among the many relics of ancient times to be seen at
Rome, are the portraits of the parents of the great St. Gregory.
The face of his father is of oval shape, rather long and grave,
with a great deal of beard; that of his mother bright and pleasant, with large blue eyes. St. Gregory was like both parents; he
had the sweetness of his mother, and the grave, earnest dignity
of his father. They were Christians, and their son was brought
up from childhood to know and love Jesus, and to lead a life
of earnest purpose. He was always fond of study, and even as
quite a young man was very learned. At the age of thirty he was
made Praetor[58] of Rome. Then his father died, and his mother
withdrew from the world and went to live in a convent, while
Gregory sold part of the lands that fell to him, in order to give
the money to endow some monasteries in Sicily. His heart was

---

58   An ancient Roman judge.

set upon doing good and living a life of usefulness. By-and-by it seemed to him that he would be better able to serve God and his fellowmen if he became a monk. So he gave up his high position in the state, laid aside the robes of silk and purple, and the glittering jewels, denied himself the good fare to which he had been used, and put on the dress and hood of a monk of the Order of St. Benedict. His grand old family palace he turned into a monastery, and at its gates built a special place called a hospice[59] to receive poor pilgrims.

One day as he was crossing the marketplace at Rome, he saw a number of little boys set out for sale! For these were the days of slavery, and the children had been taken over from Britain to be sold at Rome, where they were sure to fetch a good price—poor little lads! They had fair skins, long fair hair, and large blue eyes. Italian children are not often fair like this. Their hair is usually dark, and their eyes brown or even black. So St. Gregory was much struck by their looks, and he stopped to ask who these children were, and where they came from.

"They are Angles," was the answer. For England was then called, "Angleland," from which has come the shorter word England. "Angles," he repeated, "they ought to be angels." He thought the fair-haired, blue-eyed lads looked good and pure as must be the angels in heaven. And then he sighed to think they

---

59   A place where travelers can stay.

did not yet know even the name of the Savior, for the German tribes, from whence had come the Angles and Saxons who had conquered Britain, were known to be heathens.

"They must be taught," said St. Gregory. So he went at once and ransomed the poor little slaves, and had them taken to his monastery, where they were brought up as good Christian boys.

But Gregory was not content with putting these children in the way of salvation. He went to the Bishop of Rome—the Pope, as he is always called—and said men ought to be sent to the land across the sea from which they had come, to teach all the people there the Faith of Christ.

He begged to be allowed to go himself to the land of the Angles to preach to the people. The Pope gave leave. The few things needed for the journey were soon put together, and St. Gregory started northwards.

The journey was a very long and slow one in those early times. St. Gregory had not got very far upon his way when it became known to the people of Rome that he had left the city to go upon a distant mission. He was dearly loved by the Romans. They could not bear the thought that he had left them. No, there were plenty of monks, they said, who could be sent across the sea to the cold, distant British Islands; their own Gregory ought not to be exposed to the dangers of travel, and the trials of a life among strangers and heathens in a far-off country. Besides they could not spare him from among themselves. So some of them went to the Pope and spoke so earnestly that at last he agreed to their desire, and sent an order to St. Gregory to return to Rome.

Though he was touched by the love and attachment thus shown him by the people of his native city, St. Gregory was sorry to give up his plan; he yearned to carry the Gospel himself to the land which had given birth to those little Angle boys he had thought so like to what he fancied the angels must be. But he sent good Christian priests to England, and though he did not come in person, it is to him we owe the first Christian settlement under the Anglo-Saxons. St. Augustine was chief of the band of Missionaries who landed on the shores of Kent about the year A.D. 597, and he did his work well and zealously. In a short time, St. Gregory was made Pope. But through all his life he remained the simple, humble, hard-working, and unselfish Christian that had first won the love of the Roman people—full of learning, full of culture, but ever ready to turn his hand to the very plainest duty which came in his way.

As I have said before, those were the days of slavery. The slave trade was carried on among the nations of Europe at this time, just as it went on until almost our own times among the people of America and Africa. Men, women, and children were bought and sold by those who were rich enough to own them, as if they were mere tools. It was very rare in those days for anyone to think this wrong. But St. Gregory felt keenly how unjust it was for men, whatever their race or rank, to be treated as mere brute beasts, and all his life he preached against the custom. Slavery continued long after he had gone to his rest, but he did much to unsettle men's minds upon the subject—to make some people begin to think they were not doing right in counting among their possessions, human beings, as they counted their fields, their houses, their cattle, or their money. Perhaps many a poor slave was freed by a kind-hearted master through what the great and good St. Gregory said; and there is no doubt, since Gregory was so much loved and looked up to by all, that owners tried to act more kindly by their slaves than they would have dreamt of doing had he not spoken out so boldly what he thought. Everyone agrees that Pope Gregory did a great deal of good in his day.

He was very fond of music, and founded a school of singing. The chants we speak of as "Gregorian" are so called because it was St. Gregory who first arranged them. Often he would himself go into the choir and sit among the chorister boys, take his own part in the singing, or kindly and lovingly help them in theirs.

Though he did so much, he was never a strong man; for many years he had a weak and suffering body. But "his strength was made perfect through weakness."[60] St. Gregory died in the year A.D. 604, at the age of sixty-nine.

60   2 Corinthians 12:9

THE VENERABLE BEDE, AD 735

JETTA WOLFF

The name of Venerable Bede has indeed always been greatly honored, "venerated," both by the Church on account of St. Bede's good and holy life, and by men who love books and learning, because of the great book of history he wrote and gave to the world.

He was a north-country man, born either in Durham or Northumberland in England, and he never moved from that part of the country.

From a child Bede loved study. He was only seven years old when he was placed under the care of an Abbot named Benedict. Benedict was a man of great learning, who did all he could to bring books and treasures from other lands to England and tried to teach those around him as much and as well as was in his power. Of all the Abbot's pupils, none was like Bede, who set himself to work with his whole heart

178

and soul and became by-and-by quite the greatest scholar of his day.

It was in this monastery of Jarrow that all his life was passed. A very quiet life it was, but very busy. He seems never to have lost a moment of his time. He studied Latin and Greek, History, Medicine, and Science, besides what is called Theology, or the special learning that belongs to religion. He also gave much time to music, singing, and poetry. As quite a young man he began to teach in the great school of the monastery. Sometimes there would be six hundred pupils there at once, monks who had lived always at the convent, and strangers who came from other parts to learn of the great Bede. He loved his work. In one of the books he wrote, he says: "I always took delight in learning and teaching and writing." He speaks also of the "daily care of singing" which he had in the church. He wrote many books; the one we prize most is his Church History. It is full of stories about many good men of that time and tells us much of how people lived and thought in those days.

The story of St. Bede's last days is very beautiful. It is told us by St. Cuthbert, who was one of his pupils and was with him when he died. Even when in great pain he was bright and cheerful. "He gave thanks to God," says Cuthbert, "day and night, yea at all hours. Every day he taught us lessons, and when night after night he lay awake, he never spoke one word of complaint, but seemed only to be full of joy, and gave constant praise to God."

Through all the last days of his sickness he continued working as hard as he could with his pupils at a translation of the Gospel of St. John into English. Those about him begged he would rest. "No!" he said, "I do not want my boys to read a lie; I must see that the work is done as well as it can be before I die."

So, weak as he was, he still strove to get on with his writing, and still taught his pupils.

"Learn with what speed you may," he said to them, "I know not how long I shall last."

He grew worse. But he was eager to get on. His pupils were around him and wrote as he dictated the words. Often their own tears blinded them, and they were forced to stop, for great was the love they bore to their aged master.

On the eve of Ascension Day, St. Bede was very weak. One of his pupils, a young boy, said, "We have still one sentence left to write." "Write quickly," was the reply. Soon the boy said, "It is written;" and the master answered, "Thou hast well said—it is done, it is finished."

Then he said to the youth, "Help me to sit where I may see the place in which I was wont to kneel and pray, that so sitting I may call upon my Father."

Thus he died, leaning upon his pupil's arm, and chanting the Gloria[61]. As he chanted the word "Holy Spirit" his spirit passed from earth to heaven.

---

61   "Glory to the Father, and to the Son, and to the Holy Spirit, Both now and always, and unto the ages of ages. Amen."

S. Bonifacius.

St. Boniface, AD 755

Jetta Wolff

In the year 680 there was born in a secluded village in England, called Crediton, a little boy to whom was given the name Winfred. Among the rugged hills of his native county he grew up a strong, healthy child. We may think of him as a bright, rosy lad, tall for his age, passing the live-long day in the open air; playing with other boys in the green fields at the foot of the mountains; running with childish glee along the lanes and roadways around his village home.

Winfred was not more than five or six years old when there came, one day, a band of monks to the village. Everyone ran out to gaze upon them, and when they stopped and preached upon the village green, boys and men, women and children, all came up to hear what these strangers had to say. Among the throng was little Winfred. He listened, and his childish heart glowed. When the preaching was over, he said, "I want to be a monk like these men."

People smiled at the little fellow who was too young, they thought, even to have understood what the monks had said. But little Winfred had understood, perhaps, more than many of the older listeners, and the words of the preachers had sunk deep into the boy's heart. He knew they had spoken of a loving Savior Who had given His Life for men; of a Master Whom even a young lad as he was could serve; of a battle against all that was wrong and sinful in which each child might be a brave Christian soldier. He was not too young to have felt how hard it often is to be good, to resist what is wrong, to do what is right. The little boy of five or six had his own struggles with the evil nature within, and was able to see for himself that there was much sin among men around him. He thought nothing could be so grand and noble as to go about preaching and helping people to do right. His boyish heart was aglow, and his one wish from this day was to live among these monks and learn like them to teach and preach the Gospel.

"I too must be a monk," was his cry.

But Winfred's father would not listen to what seemed to him so strange a notion. He said sternly, "No, that cannot be." The boy was silent for the time, but as he grew older his wish grew stronger and stronger. When he was about thirteen, he was taken very ill. Everyone thought he would die. The poor father was in great trouble. What could he do to save his beloved son? He remembered the boy's wish to become a monk. He bowed his head and vowed to give up his child to God, if only his life might be spared. His prayer was not in vain. The illness passed; Winfred grew strong and well again, and the father kept his vow. The boy was sent first to the Abbey at Exeter; then he went to Nutshell, where was one of the greatest schools of those days. Winfred liked study, and he became, after a time, one of the most learned men in England. He was fond also of teaching others all that he learned and loved being among children and young people. They all loved him, too, for he was earnest and good and brave, and always full of zeal.

But St. Winfred was not content to pass his life in quiet and happiness, among duties that were easy and pleasant to him. He said he must go to the heathen and preach in rude, far-off lands the Gospel of peace and love. Across the center of Europe were vast tracts of country where the name of Christ had never been heard, where the people were wild and savage but strong and numerous; people who often made inroads upon other lands, coming in great tribes from their own forest-covered countries, and by their strength and numbers overcoming all before them. Such in those days were the Germans, two tribes of whom—the Saxons and the Angles—

had conquered a great part of Britain, as we know, about 300 years before the time of St. Winfred. To Germany, then, Winfred said he must go and work as a missionary.

In the year 716 he set out. He went first northwards to Friesland. There he worked hard for two years, teaching the people the Faith of Christ, and showing them also how to live in a less rude, rough way than was their habit.

Then he came back for a little while to England and to his monastery, of which he was made Abbot.

But St. Winfred could not rest in peace while he knew how much work there was to be done among the heathen. So he soon set out again—never to return. Before beginning his mission work this time, he went with a band of pilgrims to Rome; then he proceeded to the forest of Thuringia, where for many years he worked most bravely. It was a hard life. Often, he was in great peril, often called upon to bear cold, hunger, bodily distress of every sort. Still he went on teaching and preaching. He would never give in. After some time he left Thuringia for a little while to go again to Friesland. He found the mission he had founded there going on well, so with a thankful heart he travelled along the banks of the Rhine and the Moselle, back to Thuringia. Then he made another journey to Rome, and it was there that the new name of Boniface was given to him. So from this time he is less known by his own old English name of Winfred than by the Latin one given to him by the Pope of Rome.

To the last he wrote long and earnest letters to his friends and fellow workers in his native land. He loved England, and it must have been a great grief to him never to return there. But St. Boniface, as we will now call him, never for a moment thought of what he would like to do—only of what was his duty, of the work before him, and of what was best to be done.

The heathen among whom St. Boniface was working had in their own religion many strange rites. Like the Druids of France and Britain, they used to bow down before the great oak trees of their vast forests, and look upon them as gods, or at least as filled with power by their gods. And even when they learned to believe in Jesus Christ, they would often mix up their own strange ways of worship with the Christian prayers. St. Boniface was deeply pained at this, and thought much how he could show the people that their notions were vain and foolish.

One day he took some of his clergy, and went out into the forest of Hesse, which was near the little village of Geismar where he was staying, to cut down an immense oak tree which grew there. The Germans came round him and stood by in awe. They thought he could never cut down so huge a tree, both because of its size, and because it was sacred to the gods which they could not yet quite think false. But St. Boniface was strong of arm and will. A few strokes and the mighty oak came smashing down, split in four pieces. It seemed as if a blast of wind had suddenly swept through its branches.

Awe-struck, the heathen at once gave in. They were ready now to put aside their own rites, and worship the God of St. Boniface in simple faith. They took the beams of their grand old fallen oak and built with them a Christian oratory[62]. This was the first church of the country.

St. Boniface was not content only to turn the people from their false worship, he wished also to help them to lead settled, orderly lives. Full of bodily energy he set to work with them to make clearings in the forests, build houses and chapels, till the ground, sow, reap, fish. So they learned to love him, and to look upon the Christian saint as their true friend, and were ready to follow him in everything.

Then there came, from his English home, helpers in the great mission work. Among these were a few devoted women, sisters of the clergy. Their gentleness brought a feeling of homeliness and respect into that rude land. One of them, St. Lioba, was a cousin of Boniface. She was good and beautiful, and full of energy and helpfulness. She did much to aid the Christian work, and was of great service and comfort to St.

---

62   A place of prayer, a chapel.

Boniface and his hard-working Priests for many years.

About the year A.D. 738, St. Boniface made yet another journey to Rome. He had a glad welcome, for he had done more for Christianity than any man of his time. A hundred thousand Germans had been baptized through him. He was now made Archbishop of Mayence. For fourteen years longer he went on working as hard as when a young man. He founded six bishoprics. In history you will read that it was this St. Boniface, the Englishman Winfred, who placed the crown upon the head of Pepin le Bref when he was made King of France. But he cared little for his high position except as far as it might help him to do good for the Church of Christ. His was always the heart of a missionary, and at the age of seventy-five he begged leave of the Pope to lay aside the dignity of Archbishop, and go out once more to work as a simple monk in Friesland. He named an Englishman from Malmesbury to take his place at Mayence, and we have still the letter he wrote to the chaplain at the court of King Pepin, in which he begs the king to protect and care for the mission-workers he was leaving behind in France. Then he went forth with a band of eight brave, faithful Priests. He did not know how things would go on in Friesland; he thought it very likely he would be called on to suffer death at the hands of the heathen there, and with the few books, the Holy Gospels, and the altar-cloth which he took with him, he took also his shroud.

At first all went well. Whitsun Day came and St. Boniface pitched his tent and erected an altar in a field on the riverside. He was to hold a Confirmation that day, to lay his hands upon a number of newly baptized converts. When all was ready, he knelt in his tent in prayer until they should arrive. Poor, brave old man! Instead of the Christian converts, a fierce band of armed heathens suddenly appeared before the tent. With wild shouts they rushed upon him. His friends came up in haste, and were about to fight. St. Boniface stopped them. "We must give good for evil," he said. "I have long waited for this day: the hour of my salvation is come."

He begged his clergy to put aside their fear; with them he went out from his tent. But the heathen fell upon them with their rude wooden clubs, and soon St. Boniface was slain with all his band.

Struck down in his old age after a lifetime of devoted work, slain by those whom he had served, there he lay at rest at last, the old man who as a boy of five, listening to the Gospel story, had vowed himself to the work of a mission priest.

The heathen had expected to find booty, but there was nothing of any value to them in the tent of the saint, no vessels of gold or silver, nothing but a few books, a little wine for the Holy Communion, and some relics. They were furious, and in their anger turned and fought against each other.

Wrapped in the shroud Boniface had brought with him, the body of the saint was taken first to Maestricht, and then to Fulda, where, in time, St. Lioba was brought and laid near him.

"Sleep after toyle, port after stormie seas,

Ease after warre, death after life does greatly please."

(*Fairy Queen*, Canto IX., verse 40)

THE BATTLE OF TOURS, AD 732

ERIC WOOD

It was the eighth century, and the Saracens were over-running Western Europe; the Crescent[63] was everywhere conquering before the Cross. Caliph Abd el-Rahman, governor of Spain, mighty soldier from Africa, conqueror in Europe, led an expedition into Gaul to carry his triumphs farther. The Arabs passed through like a cyclone; and then they met Charles Martel at Tours.

Charles, surnamed Martel from the hammer-like blows which his strong arm and his armies inflicted, was Duke of the Franks. And when the Saracen peril became too pressing, and the Christian leaders found themselves helpless to combat it, Charles was called to the command of the Franks.

These latter wished to tackle the Saracens at once; Charles advised prudence, telling his followers that in their passage

---

63   The symbol of Islam.

through the country the Saracens had laid the land waste, had dismantled the monasteries of their riches and then given them to the flames; so that at every step they gained in wealth. They had, too, brought with them their families and goods to the intent to settle in the land they were about to conquer.

All these were encumbrances, as Charles knew, and he made his preparations as quickly as he could, gathering his irregular army round him, and when all was ready, marching with such haste that he came upon the Saracens between Tours and Poitiers before they expected him.

And then, in 732, was fought the Battle of Tours—the trial of strength between the Cross and the Crescent.

When Charles appeared, Abd el-Rahman was engaged in storming Tours, intent on carrying out his pillaging and burning policy. Creasy[64], translating an Arab chronicler, says: "And Abd el-Rahman and other prudent cavaliers saw the disorder of the Moslem troops, who were loaded with spoil; but they did not venture to displease the soldiers by ordering them to abandon everything except their arms and war-horses. Abd el-Rahman trusted in the valor of his soldiers, and in the good fortune which had ever attended him. But such defect of discipline is always fatal to armies. So Abd el-Rahman and his host attacked Tours to gain still

---

64   An English historian.

more spoil, and they fought against it so fiercely that they stormed the city almost before the eyes of the army that came to save it; and the fury and the cruelty of the Moslems towards the inhabitants were like the fury and cruelty of raging tigers. It was manifest that God's chastisement was sure to follow such excess."

Then came the chastisement.

The Moslems were a mighty host. Infantry from the conquered land of Spain, and wild, dashing cavalry from the deserts of Africa, veterans in the art of war, fresh from victories which had swelled their heads and filled their coffers, they looked forward to the battle with confidence. Memories of glorious battlefields filled their minds, burning towns marked their path behind them, visions of yet greater conquests rose before them; they were out to carry the Crescent throughout Europe.

As for the army of Charles Martel, it was composed of hardy men from the left bank of the Rhine, warriors from among the Franks, who had fought many a sanguine battle with the tribes who opposed the overlordship of the Hammer. Behind them lay the land which the Saracens had come to conquer; before them lay the Moslem army, and farther on, the devastated country through which the infidels had come; and each man knew that if, in the trial of strength, the Arabs won, the future held little good for the soldiers of the Cross.

Flushed with past victories, the Moslem hosts went into the fight with a rush, giving Charles no time to make the first attack. The white-robed horsemen from the desert sands swept down upon the serried ranks of Frankish warriors like a tornado. Gleaming scimitars flashed in the sun, swept round and round, and laid many a Frank low; yet still the mass held to its place, and back the Arabs were forced.

For six days did the battle thus rage, the solid wall of northmen receiving the charging cavalry at the point of the sword, "standing firm as a wall, and impenetrable as a zone of ice," but nevertheless suffering much themselves from the trampling horses and the masses of African infantry who poured down upon them and sent in their clouds of arrows. For six days neither side gained much advantage; but on the seventh day things changed.

That day the Moslems penetrated the Christian ranks, the cavalry hewing their way into the very center of the army, wielding their scimitars with deadly effect, the footmen whirling their swords round or short-thrusting them, so that Franks fell on all sides.

But weight told at last; those warriors from the north were men of iron whose battle-axes crashed through skull and body; and chief among them all was Charles the Hammer. All day the battle raged, but the Moslems could not get right through the soldiers of the Cross; they even began to doubt the issue of the battle, began to fear for the hard-won treasure in the camp.

"A false cry arose from their ranks that some of the enemy were plundering the camp; whereupon several squadrons of the Moslem horsemen rode off to protect their tents. But it seemed as if they fled; and all the host was troubled. And while Abd el-Rahman strove to check their tumult, and to lead them back to battle, the warriors of the Franks came round him, and he was pierced through with many spears so that he died. Then all the host lied before the enemy, and many died in the flight." So says the Arab chronicler.

It was an ignominious[65] retreat. Their leader slain, their treasure, so it would seem, in peril, their foe pressing hard upon them, the Arabs forgot their valor, forgot their past triumphs, forgot the purpose of their coming; and the retreat turned to a rout. Dismay seized upon their hearts; panic spread through the fleeing ranks; and, losing their heads completely, some of the Arab tribes turned their weapons upon each other.

Then the sun went down upon the scene of carnage, and the Franks drew off to wait until the morrow.

Morning came. Away in the Moslem camp not a sound was heard. What was happening? Were the Arabs lying low

---

65   Deserving of disgrace or shame.

to lure the Franks out? Charles Martel at once sent out spies to reconnoiter[66]. Carefully they made their way to the camp—and lo! it was deserted!

Under shelter of the night of the rout, the Saracens, defeated and demoralized, had fled from the field where-on they had left so many of their noblest warriors. The Cross had triumphed over the Crescent; the Hammer had swept down upon the Moslem hosts and stayed their progress through Northern Europe.

---

66   To gain information about enemy territory.

CHARLEMAGNE (CHARLES THE GREAT), AD 814

JOHN HAAREN

Charles was the most famous of the kings of the Franks. He did so many great and wonderful things that he is called Charlemagne (shar-le-main') which means Charles the Great.

He was a great soldier. For thirty years he carried on a war against the Saxons. Finally he conquered them, and their great chief, Wittekind, submitted to him. The Saxons were a people of Germany, who then lived near the land of the Franks. They spoke the same language and were of the same race as the Franks, but had not been civilized by contact with the Romans.

They were still pagans, just as the Franks had been before Clovis became a Christian. They actually offered human sacrifices.

After Charlemagne conquered them he made their lands part of his kingdom. A great number of them, among whom was Wittekind, then became Christians and were baptized;

and soon they had churches and schools in many parts of their country.

Another of Charlemagne's wars was against the Lombards. The Lombard king now invaded the Pope's lands and threatened Rome itself; so the Pope sent to Charlemagne for help. Charlemagne quickly marched across the Alps and attacked the Lombards. He drove them out of the Pope's lands and took possession of their country.

After he had conquered the Lombards he carried on war, in 778, in Spain. A large portion of Spain was then held by the Moorish Saracens. But a Mohammedan leader from Damascus had invaded their country, and the Moors invited Charlemagne to help them. He therefore led an army across the Pyrenees. He succeeded in putting his Moorish friends in possession of their lands in Spain and then set out on his return to his own country.

On the march his army was divided into two parts. The main body was led by Charlemagne himself. The rear guard was commanded by a famous warrior named Roland. While marching through the narrow pass of Roncesvalles (ron-thes-val'yes), among the Pyrenees, Roland's division was attacked by a tribe called the Basques (basks), who lived on the mountain slopes of the neighboring region.

High cliffs walled in the pass on either side. From the tops of these cliffs the Basques hurled down rocks and trunks of trees upon the Franks, and crushed many of them to death. Besides this, the wild mountaineers descended into the pass and attacked them with weapons. Roland fought bravely; but at last he was overpowered, and he and all his men were killed.

Roland had a friend and companion named Oliver, who was as brave as himself. Many stories and songs have been written telling of the wonderful adventures they were said to have had and of their wonderful deeds in war.

The work of Charlemagne in Spain was quickly undone; for Abd-er-Rahman, the leader of the Mohammedans who had come from Damascus, soon conquered almost all the territory south of the Pyrenees.

For more than forty years Charlemagne was king of the Franks; but a still greater dignity was to come to him. In the year 800 some of the people in Rome rebelled against the Pope, and Charlemagne went with an army to put down the rebellion. He entered the city with great pomp and soon conquered the rebels. On Christmas day he went to the church of St. Peter, and as he knelt before the altar the Pope placed a crown upon his head, saying:

"Long live Charles Augustus, Emperor of the Romans."

The people assembled in the church shouted the same words; and so Charlemagne was now emperor of the Western Roman Empire, as well as king of the Franks. [Note: The emperors of Constantinople still called themselves Roman Emperors, and still claimed Italy, Germany and France as parts of their empire, though really their authority had not been respected in these countries for more than 300 years.]

Charlemagne built a splendid palace at Aix-la-Chapelle (aks-la-shap-el'), a town in Germany, where perhaps he was born.

Charlemagne was a tall man, with long, flowing beard, and of noble appearance. He dressed in very simple style; but when he went into battle he wore armor, as was the custom for kings and nobles, and often for ordinary soldiers in his day.

Armor was made of leather or iron, or both together. There was a helmet of iron for the head, and a breastplate to cover the breast, or a coat of mail to cover the body. The coat of mail was made of small iron or steel rings linked together, or fastened on to a leather shirt. Coverings for the legs and feet were often attached to the coat.

Charlemagne was a great king in many other ways besides the fighting of battles. He did much for the good of his people. He made many excellent laws and appointed judges to see that the laws were carried out. He established schools and placed good teachers in charge of them. He had a school in his palace for his own children, and he employed as their teacher a very learned Englishman named Alcuin.

In those times few people could read or write. There were not many schools anywhere, and in most places there were none at all. Even the kings had little education. Indeed, few of them could write their own names, and most of them did not care about sending their children to school. They did not think that reading or writing was of much use; but thought that it was far better for boys to learn to be good soldiers, and for girls to learn to spin and weave.

Charlemagne had a very different opinion. He was fond of learning; and whenever he heard of a learned man, living in any foreign country, he tried to get him to come and live in Frankland.

The fame of Charlemagne as a great warrior and a wise emperor spread all over the world. Many kings sent messengers to him to ask his friendship, and bring him presents. Harun-al-Rashid (hah-roon' al rash'-eed), the famous caliph, who lived at Bagdad, in Asia, sent him an elephant and a clock which struck the hours. The Franks were much astonished at the sight of the elephant; for they had never seen one before. They also wondered much at the clock. In those days there were in Europe no clocks such as we have; but water-clocks and hour-glasses were used in some places. The water-clock was a vessel into which water was allowed to trickle. It contained a float which pointed to a scale of hours at the side of the vessel.

The float gradually rose as the water trickled in.

The hour-glasses measured time by the falling of fine sand from the top to the bottom of a glass vessel made with a narrow neck in the middle for the sand to go through. They were like the little glasses called egg-timers, which are used for measuring the time for boiling eggs.

Charlemagne died in 814. He was buried in the church which he had built at Aix-la-Chapelle. His body was placed in the tomb, seated upon a grand chair, dressed in royal robes, with a crown on the head, a sword at the side, and a Bible in the hands.

This famous emperor is known in history as Charlemagne, which is the French word for the German name Karl der Grosse (Charles the Great), the name by which he was called at his own court during his life. The German name would really be a better name for him; for he was a German, and German was the language that he spoke. The common name of his favorite residence, Aix-la-Chapelle, also is French, but he knew the place as Aachen (ä'chen).

The great empire which Charlemagne built up held together only during the life of his son. Then it was divided among his three grandsons. Louis took the eastern part, Lo-thaire' took the central part, with the title of emperor, and Charles took the western part.

AELFREDUS
MAGNUS

ALFRED THE GREAT, AD 899

JOHN HAAREN

The Danes were neighbors of the Norwegian Vikings, and like them were fond of the sea and piracy. They plundered the English coasts for more than a century; and most of northern and eastern England became for a time a Danish country with Danish kings.

What saved the rest of the country for the Saxons was the courage of the great Saxon king, Alfred.

Alfred was the son of Ethelwulf, king of the West Saxons. He had a loving mother who brought him up with great care. Up to the age of twelve, it is said, he was not able to read well, in spite of the efforts of his mother and others to teach him.

When Alfred was a boy there were no printed books. The wonderful art of printing was not invented until about the year 1440—nearly six hundred years later than Alfred's time. Moreover, the art of making paper had not yet been invented. Consequently the few books in use in Alfred's time were written by skillful penmen, who wrote generally on leaves of parchment, which was sheepskin carefully prepared so that it might retain ink.

One day Alfred's mother showed him and his elder brothers a beautiful volume which contained a number of the best Saxon ballads. Some of the words in this book were written in brightly colored letters, and upon many of the leaves were painted pictures of gaily-dressed knights and ladies.

"Oh, what a lovely book!" exclaimed the boys.

"Yes, it is lovely," replied the mother. "I will give it to whichever of you children can read it the best in a week."

Alfred began at once to take lessons in reading and studied hard day after day. His brothers passed their time in amusements and made fun of Alfred's efforts. They thought he could not learn to read as well as they could, no matter how hard he should try.

At the end of the week the boys read the book to their mother, one after the other. Much to the surprise of his brothers, Alfred proved to be the best reader and his mother gave him the book.

While still very young Alfred was sent by his father to Rome to be anointed by His Holiness, the Pope. It was a long and tiresome journey, made mostly on horseback.

With imposing, solemn ceremony he was anointed by the Holy Father. Afterwards he spent a year in Rome receiving religious instruction.

In the year 871, when Alfred was twenty-two years old, the Danes invaded various parts of England. Some great battles were fought, and Alfred's elder brother Ethelred, king of the West Saxons, was killed. Thus Alfred became king.

The Danes still continued to fight the Saxons, and defeated Alfred in a long and severe struggle. They took for themselves the northern and eastern parts of England.

Moreover, Danes from Denmark continued to cross the sea and ravage the coast of Saxon England. They kept the people in constant alarm. Alfred therefore determined to meet the pirates on their own element, the sea. So he built and equipped the first English navy, and in 875 gained the first naval victory ever won by the English.

A few years after this, however, great numbers of Danes from the northern part of England came pouring into the Saxon lands. Alfred himself was obliged to flee for his life.

For many months he wandered through forests and over hills to avoid being taken by the Danes. He sometimes made his home in caves and in the huts of shepherds and cowherds. Often he tended the cattle and sheep and was glad to get a part of the farmer's dinner in pay for his services.

Once, when very hungry, he went into the house of a cow-herd and asked for something to eat. The cowherd's wife was baking cakes and she said she would give him some when they were done.

"Watch the cakes and do not let them burn, while I go across the field to look after the cows," said the woman, as she hurried away. Alfred took his seat on the chimney-corner to do as he was told. But soon his thoughts turned to his troubles and he forgot about the cakes.

When the woman came back she cried out with vexation, for the cakes were burned and spoiled. "You lazy, good-for-nothing man!" she said, "I warrant you can eat cakes fast enough; but you are too lazy to help me bake them."

With that she drove the poor hungry Alfred out of her house. In his ragged dress he certainly did not look like a king, and she had no idea that he was anything but a poor beggar.

Some of Alfred's friends discovered where he was hiding and joined him. In a little time a body of soldiers came to him and a strong fort was built by them. From this fort Alfred and his men went out now and then and gave battle to small parties of the Danes. Alfred was successful and his army grew larger and larger.

One day he disguised himself as a wandering minstrel and went into the camp of the Danes. He strolled here and there, playing on a harp and singing Saxon ballads. At last, Guthrum, the commander of the Danes, ordered the minstrel to be brought to his tent.

Alfred went. "Sing to me some of your charming songs," said Guthrum. "I never heard more beautiful music." So the kingly harper played and sang for the Dane, and went away with handsome presents. But better than that, he had gained information that was of the greatest value.

In a week he attacked the Danish forces and defeated them with great slaughter in a battle which lasted all day and far into the night. Guthrum was taken prisoner and brought before Alfred.

Taking his harp in his hands, Alfred played and sang one of the ballads with which he had entertained Guthrum in the camp. The Dane started in amazement and exclaimed:

"You, then, King Alfred, were the wandering minstrel?"

"Yes," replied Alfred, "I was the musician whom you received so kindly. Your life is now in my hands; but I will give you your liberty if you will become a Christian and never again make war on my people."

"King Alfred," said Guthrum, "I will become a Christian, and so will all my men if you will grant liberty to them as to me; and henceforth, we will be your friends."

Alfred then released the Danes, and they were baptized as Christians.

An old road running across England from London to Chester was then agreed upon as the boundary between the Danish and Saxon kingdoms; and the Danes settled in East Anglia, as the eastern part of England was called.

Years of peace and prosperity followed for Alfred's kingdom. During these years the king rebuilt the towns that had been destroyed by the Danes, erected new forts, and greatly strengthened his army and navy.

He also encouraged trade; and he founded a school like that established by Charlemagne. He himself translated a number of Latin books into Saxon, and probably did more for the cause of education than any other king that ever wore the English crown.

THE FIRST CRUSADE, AD 1096-1099

E.M. WILMOT-BUXTON

The countries round about the Holy Land began to be harassed by a new and terrible foe. From far-off Turkestan had migrated a fierce fighting tribe, the descendants of one Seljuk, and known to history as the Seljukian Turks. Wherever they went they conquered, until half-way through the eleventh century, their leader drove out the Saracen rulers of Bagdad and made himself Caliph.

His successor was converted to Islam, and with added power, swept over Asia Minor and settled in the city of Nicaea, in threatening proximity to Constantinople.

This invasion was the more terrible in that it brought in its train a relapse to barbarism, for these Turks were barbarians, hordes of robbers and brigands, who cared for nothing but plunder and violence.

Alexios, the Emperor of the Eastern Empire, quailed at

their approach, and looked on in terror at the spectacle of Christian churches destroyed and Christian children sold into slavery. But he appealed in vain for aid to the kingdom of the West. To unite Western Christendom against a far-off foe was a task beyond the powers of the tottering Empire of the East.

That inspiration, however, was at hand. In 1076, the Seljukian Turks conquered Jerusalem, and at once began a reign of terror for Christian inhabitants and pilgrims. The Patriarch, or Bishop of Jerusalem, was dragged through the street by his white hair, and flung into a dungeon, until his people could gather a sum sufficient to pay his ransom. The holiest sacrament of the Church was profaned by the barbarians, who invaded the buildings and insisted upon sharing in the rite. Pilgrims were stripped and beaten on the roads and passes that led to the Holy City; many suffered martyrdom as they knelt before the Holy Tomb. Out of seven thousand who set out from Germany in one year, only two thousand returned to tell a tale of cruel murder and outrage. The marvel is that such a terrible state of things was allowed to exist so long, without anything being done to remedy it. Pope Gregory VII. (Hildebrand) did indeed gather an army in the latter part of the eleventh century, but his energy was dissipated in the hopeless task of asserting the power of the Pope over the Emperor, and his army was eventually dispersed.

Robert Guiscard, the Norman, actually crossed the sea with his troops in 1081, when death overtook him; and for a time the unhappy pilgrims seemed to be left to their fate. Then suddenly was heard a "voice calling in the wilderness," the voice of one who was to be the herald of the First Crusade.

The story goes that a certain poor hermit named Peter, a native of the French city of Amiens, set out to go to Jerusalem in the year 1093. He had, like everyone else, heard of the horrors he might be called upon to endure, but pushed on, undeterred, until, possibly because of his poverty, he arrived safely within the Holy City. He found the condition of things even worse than he expected. The very stones of the great church were stained with the blood of the martyrs; the cries of tortured women rang in his ears; the patriarch Simeon confessed that he had lost heart and was little better than a slave in the Moslem's hands. It was clear that the Emperor of the East, their proper protector, would never act up to his responsibilities. To whom, then, could they look for aid?

"The nations of the West shall take up arms in your cause," cried the dauntless Peter, and he forthwith promised to visit the Pope and obtain his help and sympathy on his return journey, if the Patriarch would give him letters to the Church of Rome.

The Hermit at once hurried to the coast and sailed for Italy. He came before Pope Urban II at the very time when the envoys of the Emperor of Constantinople were knocking very hard at the doors of Rome. Urban therefore did not hesitate to bless the enterprise of Peter, and to bid him go forth and preach a Crusade in his own way.

To induce kings, princes, and nobles, to leave their lands and go to fight in a cause from which they could gain no apparent profit, needed considerable time, and Urban himself undertook the difficult task. But he was wise enough to see that the peculiar power of Peter the Hermit could be used in stirring up the ordinary people, the simple-minded and the poor, to take up arms for the cause of Christ. So, as a writer of his own time puts it. "The hermit set out, from whence I know not, but we saw him passing through the towns and villages, preaching everywhere, and the people surrounding him in crowds, loading him with offerings and celebrating his sanctity with such great praises that I never remember such honor bestowed on anyone."

Throughout Italy and France and along the banks of the Rhine journeyed the strange inspired figure, with head and feet bare, his thin frame wrapped in a coarse cloak, holding before him a great crucifix as he rode upon an ass.

"He preached to innumerable crowds in the churches, the streets and the highways; the Hermit entered with equal confidence the palace and the cottage; and the people were impetuously moved by his call to repentance and to arms. When he painted the sufferings of the natives and pilgrims of Palestine, every heart was melted to compassion; every breast glowed with indignation when he challenged the warriors of the age to defend their brethren and rescue their Savior."

While Southern Europe was thus being stirred to enthusiasm by being brought into personal contact with one who had seen for himself the woes of the Holy Land, Pope Urban had already called a council to consider the matter in a practical form. At this Council of Placentia, however, the chief part of the attention of those present was drawn to the representations of the Greek Emperor, on whose behalf ambassadors pleaded the cause of the city of Constantinople. If that city fell before the threatened onslaught of the Turks, they said, Christianity must perish forever in the East, and nothing but a narrow stretch of sea kept the Moslems from the gates of the capital city of the Eastern Empire.

At these words the deepest sympathy was expressed, but it was suggested that the best way of succoring[67] the threatened city was to draw off the attention of the Turks by an attack upon Palestine itself. This was just what Urban desired. A definite march upon Jerusalem would fire the imaginations of men of all ranks far more than an attempt to defend Constantinople

---

67   To give assistance or aid.

before it was actually besieged. The old jealousy between the Eastern and Western Empire had to be reckoned with. The whole question, was, therefore, deferred until the autumn of 1095, when a Council was summoned at Clermont in France.

That dull November day witnessed a most striking scene. The vast open square in front of the Cathedral was crammed with people of all classes drawn from all quarters by the rumor that the subject of a Crusade would be discussed. From the great western door, immediately after High Mass, emerged the figure of the Pope, and a number of bishops and cardinals, dressed in vestments glowing with color, followed him upon the high scaffold covered with red cloth.

With cross outstretched in his left hand, the Pope held up his right to command attention, and then began to speak. "Who can preserve the force of that eloquence?" says one who stood by, and heard him point out that the Turks, having pushed their way to the edge of the Western World, and even then holding parts of Spain, must now be driven forth from that holiest place.

Turning to the knights who stood by, leaning upon their swords, Urban addressed them in words of fire.

"Were they spending their days in empty quarrels, shearing their brethren like sheep? Let them go forth and fight boldly for the Cause of God. Christ himself would be their leader as, more valiant than the Israelites of old, they fought for their Jerusalem. A goodly thing would it be for them to die in that city, where Christ for them laid down His life. Let them, as valiant knights, descendants of unconquered sires, remember the vigor of their ancestors and go forth to conquer or to die."

This appeal stirred the multitude to its depths.

"DEUS VULT! DEUS VULT!" went up to heaven in one great roar of voices, and the cry was at once seized upon by Urban.

"Let these words be your war-cry," he exclaimed. "When you attack the enemy, let the words resound from every side, 'God wills it' Go forth then; many sufferings will be yours, but you may redeem your souls at the expense of your bodies. Rid God's sanctuary of the wicked; expel the robbers; bring in the holy souls. These things I command, and for their carrying out I fix the end of next spring. If you have rich possessions here, you are promised better ones in the Holy Land. Those who die will enter the mansions of heaven, while the living shall behold the sepulcher of their Lord. Ye are soldiers of the Cross; wear then on your breasts, or on your shoulders, the blood-red sign of Him who died for the salvation of your souls. Wear it as a token that His help will never fail you; wear it as a pledge of a vow which can never be recalled."

Another mighty burst of applause followed these words.

Crowds of bishops and knights at once pressed forward to take the red cross badges which had been prepared, and Adhemar, Bishop of Puy, the first to do so, was at once appointed as spiritual head of the expedition, with Raymond, Count of Toulouse, as its military leader.

In the months that followed, all Southern Europe rang with the sounds of riveting armor and of forging steel. The actual departure of the Crusaders had been finally appointed for the August of 1096.

It was with high hearts that the remnant of the crusading host, now much reduced, took the road to the Holy City, the end of all their endeavors. With some difficulty they made their way along the smiling plain of the River Orontes, and then keeping close to the coastline between the mountains of Libanus and the sea, passed through the famous cities of Tyre, Sidon, and Joppa.

From the last of these they turned inland, and taking possession of the little town of Ramleh, supposed to be the burial place of St George, the patron saint of England, the leaders held a council to consider their next movements.

Those who cared most for the mere worldly success of the undertaking were now strongly of opinion that they should leave Jerusalem untouched for the present and attack the true centers of the power of Islam, Babylon and Alexandria. Others reminded these men of the real object of the Crusades and asked scoffingly how they hoped to seize great and populous cities if they could not first capture the little town of Jerusalem. The worldly-minded gave way, but consoled themselves by capturing villages and farms on the route of march. The rest, more serious minded, "set their faces steadfastly to go towards Jerusalem." "And those to whom the Lord's command was dearer than lust of gain, advanced with naked feet, sighing heavily for the disdain that the others showed for the Lord's command."

Whilst resting at Emmaus at nightfall of June 6, 1099, a little band of Christians living at Bethlehem crept into the camp and told the leaders a doleful story of the cruelty and oppression of Islam. The information that the birthplace of the Lord was near at hand quickened every pulse. Sleep was forgotten, and a hurried march begun which brought them in a few hours to the top of Mount Mizpeh, whence, with swelling hearts, they watched the sun rise upon the sacred walls of the Holy City.

"Jerusalem! Jerusalem!"

The cry, restrained and reverent, filled the morning air, as the great host fell prostrate and kissed the hallowed soil.

By its natural position the city was exceedingly difficult to take by assault, for it stood upon a rocky plateau, guarded by the two steep valleys of Kedron and Hinnon.

It was, moreover, defended by about forty thousand picked Saracen warriors—a band equal in number to that of the besiegers, but possessing far greater advantages as to position and supplies.

With the utmost confidence, however, the Crusaders took up their posts. Robert of Normandy being stationed on the north, Godfrey of Bouillon and Tancred on the west, while Count Raymond advanced to Mount Sion on the south.

It was clear from the first assault that they had undertaken no light task, and meantime the usual horrors of famine and thirst made their appearance in the camp. There was little shade in that region; the groves around had been cut down to provide wood for the "machines of war," and the chief water supply—a spring which bubbled up every other day—was soon choked by the corpses of men and beasts who had trodden one another down in the wild attempt to obtain drink.

The springs further off had all been poisoned by the Saracens, and when the supplies of fruit began to fail, it seemed as though the army would never possess the strength to attack the city again.

A still worse calamity was the quarrelling which now broke out again among the leaders. Tancred was bitterly censured for having set up his banner over the Church of the Nativity at Bethlehem, Raymond for having taken to himself the post of honor on the sacred Mount of Sion. The rank and file, following the example of their chiefs, gave themselves over to laxity, disobedience, and personal feuds.

Once again it was necessary to invigorate the faith of the Crusaders, and accordingly Peter the Hermit declared that the dead Adhemar had appeared to him with words of severe rebuke for the sins of the camp, and the promise that the city should fall if the army would march barefoot round it for the space of nine days. A council was summoned, at which the noble Tancred was the first to make up a long-standing quarrel with Count Raymond; a feeling of good-will and reconciliation was spread abroad; and it was determined to make a fresh attempt in a spirit of more fervid religious zeal.

On the 12th of July 1099, while the Saracens were setting up crucifixes upon the ramparts and insulting their Christian foes by spitting and throwing mud upon them, a solemn procession, fully armed, singing psalms and litanies, made its way around the walls; and a sermon preached from the Mount of Olives by Arnulf, the future Bishop of Jerusalem, roused even the most despondent.

On the next two days, Wednesday and Thursday, assaults were made, but without much success. On the Friday the Crusaders, having been reminded that it was the day of the Lord's

Passion and Death, came to the work with new vigor, "even the women and the children," writes the historian, "were eager to do their part on that field."

But when Count Raymond fought on the south of the city it seemed as though success was hopeless. His wooden tower, which protected the archers, was burnt by the throwing of flaming oil from the walls, and his men were driven into utter confusion. Suddenly, when retreat seemed inevitable, a marvelous portent was seen. On the Mount of Olives, on the further side of the city, appeared a knight in glittering armor, waving a flaming sword over Jerusalem. The rumor quickly spread that it was St George come to the aid of the Crusaders. "Deus vult! Deus vult!" they shouted, and in the vigor of their assault the outer wall was won.

The explanation of the occurrence was soon clear. At the further side of the city the stone-slingers of Godfrey of Boulogne had at length driven the Saracens from the ramparts. Seizing and lowering the drawbridge, and scrambling up the walls by scaling ladders, the Teuton host, headed by Bernard of St Valery, leapt upon the battlements. A certain unknown knight waved his sword in signal of victory from the top of Mount Olives, and this had been the sign which put new heart into Count Raymond's men.

At the very hour at which their Savior breathed His dying words upon the Cross, the red-cross standard was first seen to float over the walls of the Holy City.

From the horrors of bloodshed that followed the capture of Jerusalem we can but turn away in disgust. "Such a slaughter of pagan folk had never been seen or heard of; none know their number save God alone."

After that scene of slaughter and violence the leaders of the Crusaders walked, bareheaded and barefooted, dressed in long white mantles marked with the red cross, to the Church of the Holy Sepulcher to offer thanks for their success. Amongst them stood Peter the Hermit, the real moving spirit of the Crusade, in spite of his mistaken zeal as a leader of men.

It is said that many of the Christian inhabitants of the city recognized him as the unknown pilgrim who had promised to rouse on their behalf the nations of the west, and they clung to his raiment with tears of gratitude. It is the last glimpse we have of that enthusiastic personality, and we may be content to leave him there, at the moment when his great aim had been accomplished.

ST. FRANCIS OF ASSISI, AD 1226

GEORGE HODGES

Of all the merry lads in the sunny streets of Assisi, the merriest was young Francis Bernadone. He it was who sang the liveliest songs, and wore the brightest clothes, and was the leader of the games. His father was a merchant whose shop was filled with silk and cloth of gold, and there was money for Francis to spend, and he spent it splendidly. He worked, too, in the shop, and carried his father's goods into the market of Assisi, and into other markets, even so far away as Rome.

Assisi stands on a hilltop and looks out over some of the fairest fields of Italy. One can also away to Perugia on another hilltop, with whose citizens the Assisans used to fight whenever opportunity offered. It was thus made plain to Francis, even from the beginning of his life, that Assisi was not the whole of the world. And this important fact, by his journeys into other towns, he confirmed. In one of the battles with Perugia he was

S.<small>T</small> FRANÇOIS.

François dans la priere, et dans la penitence
Passe en ce triste lieu des jours delicieux:
L'image de la mort flate son esperance,
Il n'atache qu'au ciel ses desirs, et ses yeux.

a Paris chez Joullain Quay de la Megisserie a la Ville de Rome taken captive and lay for a whole year in a Perugian prison. Thus amidst his merriment, he had time to think.

One day, in Rome, going into St. Peter's Church, and noticing there the careful economy with which the worshipers made their offerings to God, he took his purse and threw down all he had before an altar, the gold and silver making a great clattering upon the floor. Then he changed clothes with a beggar on the church steps, and there sat all day and begged.

Twice, after an illness, he dreamed strange dreams which seemed to tell him what he ought to do with his life.

One was the vision of a great armory full of swords and lances, into which he was bidden to go and arm himself. He thought that this meant that he should be a soldier, and out he started on the next expedition, with shield and helmet, mounted on horseback. But he came back, convinced that soldiering was not the trade for him.

The other dream commanded him to rebuild a ruined church, and at once he set about the work of making a new wall for the little chapel of St. Darnian. He went around asking his neighbors to give him stones.

It was this rebuilding of St. Darnian's which sent Francis finally upon his great career. The repairing even of a small, ruined church without money, and with no other labor than that of one pair of unaccustomed hands, is a slow process.

Francis grew impatient. One day, filled with a great desire to get on with this good work, he took a lot of bales of cloth out of his father's store, and rode away to the next town, and sold both cloth and horse. "There," he said to the priest of St. Darnian's, "take this money for the church." But the priest was not willing to take it, fearing the displeasure of Francis's father. Francis, too, as he considered the matter, began to see that his father might object to this selling of his goods. He tossed the money into a corner and hid himself. And, indeed, his father did object most seriously. His neighbors also felt that Francis had done wrong. When, at last, he ventured out of hiding and made his way to his home, they hooted him in the streets, said he was crazy, and stoned him, till, as he drew near the house, his father came out to see what all the noise might mean, and, finding Francis, seized him, dragged him in, and locked him up.

Francis was not a boy when these events took place. He was twenty-five years old. Of course, it was not right for him to take things out of his father's store and sell them, even for the Church, but he naturally felt, after years of service, that the business belonged in part to him. Anyhow, he was not penitent[68], and one day when his mother, in love and pity, let him out, back he went to St. Darnian's.

---

68   Showing remorse or regret.

And then his father went to law about it. He appealed to the magistrates to get his money back. The matter was referred to the bishop. The bishop wisely advised the young man to restore the money to his father; and this he did, gathering it up from the dusty corner where he had thrown it. But when he brought it to his father, he brought his clothes also. He took off his fine garments, piled them on the floor and put the money on top. "Now," he cried, "I am the servant of God, and my father is the Father who is in heaven."

The bishop flung a cloak about him, and somebody gave him clothes to wear, and his lodging was at St. Darnian's. The good priest gave him food, and, mindful of the rich feasts in which he had delighted, gave him some dainties with it. For Francis, who was always a boy to the end of his life, confessed long after that he had never lost his early liking for sweet things. But when Francis saw the dainties, he perceived that he had not even yet given up the luxuries of life. Immediately, he took a plate and went out and begged his food from door to door.

From that moment, Francis was independently poor. Gradually, companions came to him, first one and then another, wishing to share his life, and he required them all to give up everything that they possessed. The idea of a great society had not come into his mind, but it was plain already that for himself and his little company of friends, poverty was the best condition. In an age which was tremendously intent on money, when even the Church was more anxious to be rich than to be holy, there was a need of men who had no interest in wealth. These men cared nothing for it. They were glad to be poor. They were happy to be the brothers of the poor. They went about begging with the beggars.

One day, in church, Francis heard the words of Christ to His disciples, telling them to provide no money for their journey, and to take with them neither shoes, nor staff, nor wallet, but to go and preach, saying, "The kingdom of heaven is at hand."[69] Immediately, he took the words as meant for him. He cast away his shoes and his staff; he unloosed the girdle from which his wallet was suspended, and finding a rope, tied it about his brown cloak. Thus the new order was provided with a uniform. They went with bare feet, in cloak of brown tied with a rope. And they began to preach. They journeyed about among the little towns of Umbria, getting people together in market-places, and speaking to them concerning God and their souls.

One of the beautiful stories of the preaching of Francis is about his sermon to the birds. As he was preaching to the people, the birds came and made such a noise chirping to each other in the air that the voice of the speaker could hardly be heard. Then the saint, with his gentle courtesy, turned to the birds.

69   Luke 10:1-9

"My sisters," he said, "it is now time that I should speak. Since you have had your say, listen now in your turn to the word of God, and be silent till the sermon is finished." And the legend says that the birds obeyed, and sat still, listening with attention.

Another time, when the number of the disciples of Francis had grown great, and the Little Brothers, as they called themselves, were very many, they held a council at Assisi, in the flowery plain beside the church of St. Mary of the Angels. But Francis had made no arrangements for feeding his multitude of guests. "My children," he said, "we have promised great things to God, and greater things still have we promised ourselves from God; let us observe those which we have promised to Him, and certainly expect those which are promised to us." And from all the neighboring towns people came driving in with food, so that they had more than enough.

One day Francis said to a young brother of the company, "Let us go into the town and preach." So in they went from St.

Mary's church beside the gate, and climbed the long Assisi hill, and went about the streets and markets, and at last turned their steps towards home having said never a word. At last the young man asked, "Father, when do we begin to preach?" And Francis answered, "My son, we have been preaching all the way, for men have seen us as we went, and we have been sermons without speech. Every man is a sermon every day."

One dark night Francis and Leo walked in the cold rain, weary after a long journey, Francis before, Leo behind. And Francis said, "Brother Leo, if we were able to give sight to the blind and hearing to the deaf and recovery to the sick, that would not be the perfect joy." And presently Francis said, "Brother Leo, if we were able to know all knowledge, that would not be the perfect joy." And, a while after Francis said, "Brother Leo, if we were able to speak with the tongues of angels, that would not be the perfect joy." "Well then, Father Francis," said Leo at last, "what would be the perfect joy?" And Francis answered, "Here we come, dripping with rain, and shivering with cold, to the monastery of St. Mary of the Angels, expecting dry clothes, and warmth and food and sleep. Suppose the porter does not know us. We knock, and he says, 'Who is there?' and we answer, 'We are two of thy brethren,' and he says, 'You are two vagabonds, you are two tramps,' and out he comes and beats us, and calls us hard names, and rolls

us in the mud and snow, and goes in, fastening the door behind him. Then if we get up and go on in great content, glad to
suffer hardships, remembering how our Master suffered for our
sake, that, Brother Leo, would be the perfect joy."

These stories illustrate the character of Francis. He was the
most gentle, the most cheerful, the most unselfish of the saints.
In the midst of a time when every man seemed to be thinking
chiefly of his own advantage, Francis sought no gain whatever, and desired only to be of service to others. His example
revealed the fact that the world was not so selfish as it seemed.
Not only were there men who came to live under his rule,
but great numbers of women, beginning with Clara, a devout
young girl of Assisi, who came from her pleasant home to
follow the brown-gowned brethren, and took up her residence
in that little church of St. Darnian which Francis had rebuilt.
And after her, in the enthusiasm which a holy life enkindled,
came multitudes of men and women having still their business in the world, their shops to keep, their children to bring
up, unable to live in the complete consecration and poverty of
Francis and Clara, and yet most earnestly desiring to be better.
And for them Francis established a third order, giving them
simple rules of devout living which they could keep in their
own homes. Thus the influence of Francis began to touch all
the life about him.

He went to Rome, to ask the blessing of the pope upon his new society. It is said that the great Innocent, who had humbled the king of England, was walking in his garden when Francis appeared, and at first ordered him away, thinking that he was a beggar from the street who had got in by mistake; but it was the pope who was mistaken. Innocent blessed the work of Francis, as he was presently to bless the work of Dominic.

He went even to the remote East, to Egypt and the Holy Land, following the track of the Crusaders, and had an interview with the Sultan. The Sultan was engaged in killing Christians, but Francis was not afraid. In he went and preached his gospel, to which the Sultan listened gravely, and dismissed him in peace.

And year by year, the influence of the self-sacrifice of Francis extended, and the Order grew. One day, the report was brought to him that in a certain city a generous man had given some of his followers a house to live in. He was filled with great grief and alarm. He foresaw that his disciples, devoted to holy poverty and friends of the people because they were poor as the poorest, would by-and-by grow rich like the rest of them, like the men who had followed Benedict, and the men who had followed Bernard. And so indeed it proved. Even in his own lifetime, the beautiful simplicity of the Order began to be changed.

On he went, walking in the steps of Jesus, making his life as near as he could like the perfect life. He went singing, with the love songs of the spirit in place of the love songs of the troubadours. The sun and moon, the hills and lakes, the birds and beasts, he called his brothers and sisters, and made a poem about them, praising God for all the blessings of the world. He was always kind and tender, courteous and gentle; but never sparing himself. Even near the end of his short life, when sickness had begun to overtake him, he would say, "Let us begin over again; up to this moment we have done nothing for God."

SANCTA ELISABETH

238

St. Elizabeth of Hungary, AD 1231

Theodor Berthold

St. Elizabeth was the daughter of King Andrew II of Hungary and was born in the year 1207. The little princess was carried to her baptism followed by a grand procession. She was most carefully trained and taught, and from her earliest childhood she loved God and the poor.

When she was barely four years old, she was taken away from her parents to live among strangers. You will ask why? My dear children, in those days it was the custom to promise children in marriage at their birth or soon after. So Elizabeth was promised to Louis, the son of the landgrave[70] of Thuringia, in Germany. With an escort of many nobles, of horsemen, and of servants, Elizabeth was taken to the Wartburg[71] near Eisenach. Here Eliza-

---

70   The title of a German prince.
71   A castle in Thuringia, Germany.

beth and Louis were solemnly betrothed, and were then raised together.

The noisy life at the castle of the landgrave did not prevent Elizabeth from giving up her childish heart to Our Lord. Prayer and self-denial were her constant occupations. Even in her play she kept God in mind, and the least shadow of impurity was shunned by her. She had no mind for pride of dress and display

In her childhood Elizabeth took particular delight in temporal and spiritual works of mercy. She always gave her pin-money[72] to the poor, with the hope that they would say a prayer for her. She gathered up the food left over from meals and gave it to the hungry. Once she went to a cemetery with her playmates. There she said to them: "The people who are buried here were once living, as we are. Now they are dead, as we will someday be. Therefore, we should love God. And now please say after me: Christ, through Thy bitter death and through Thy dear Mother Mary, deliver the souls, and give us who are living Thy grace, that we may attain to the eternal joy of heaven."

As long as the landgrave lived, things were pleasant for Elizabeth. After his death his widow Sophia and her daughter Agnes, who were both worldly minded and lax in religious matters, made it very hard for Elizabeth. Because she liked to

---

72   An allowance or pocket money.

serve the poor, these ladies called her a servant and not a princess. Even the nobility made fun of her. She was like a lamb among wolves. They even tried to turn Louis, her promised husband, against her. They told him to send her to a convent. But in vain, for Louis valued her angelic patience and her piety.

In her fifteenth year she was married. Elizabeth was very happy with her young husband, and he, being a most God-fearing man, allowed her to go on with her pious practices. She visited the sick, helped the needy, and would spin and weave clothing for the poor with her own hands. As an angel of mercy she appeared in the humble homes which she visited. The many roses blooming on the Wartburg keep the memory of the lovely miracle of roses fresh to this day. Once when Elizabeth had a basket of food for the poor under her cloak, her husband stopped her and asked what she had there. Blushing to tell her own charity, she answered, "Roses to weave a wreath for myself." He asked to see them, and when he turned back her cloak the basket was full of roses.

A famine which desolated Thuringia in 1225 and caused great misery gave Elizabeth opportunity to increase her charity. She built two hospitals and fed nine hundred poor every day. At that time there were many lepers. Everyone shrank in disgust from these poor wretches, but not Elizabeth. She loved them for Christ's sake. With her own hands she bathed them, and combed their hair, sat with them, and cheered and encouraged them to trust and hope in God.

After Elizabeth had had six years of happiness, the Lord put a heavy trial upon her. Her beloved husband died in a crusade in which he had joined with other Christian princes for the rescue of the Holy Land. His brother Henry usurped his place and turned Elizabeth with her four young children out of the Wartburg. It was in the middle of winter, and the outcast princess was not permitted to take a thing with her. The daughter of a king was poorer than the poorest beggar, for the new lord of the land had even forbidden his subjects to give her and her hungry and freezing children shelter and food. At last an innkeeper near Eisenach gave the wanderers leave to sleep in his stable. And here the princess and her children were glad to take refuge. When the midnight bell of the Franciscan Church called the brothers to matins the saint went to the church and asked the brothers to sing the Te Deum in thanksgiving that she was vouchsafed[73] to find shelter in a stable, even as Mary had been in Bethlehem.

Elizabeth went from Eisenach to Bamberg, where her uncle took her under his protection. He was the Bishop of Bamberg and succeeded in persuading her brother-in-law to give back the city of Marburg and its revenues to Elizabeth. Elizabeth

---

73   Granted as a special favor.

forgave her brother-in-law and never spoke a word of blame against him, but she did not want to know anything more of the world. She chose a hut outside of Marburg for her dwelling and took the habit of the Third Order of St. Francis on Good Friday of the year 1229. Her beloved children she gave up for the sake of Christ after having arranged for their right education and training, and she herself lived only for prayer, work, and the care of the sick. She gave all her income to the poor, and lived only on bread and meat cooked in water.

On the 19th of November, 1231, her pure soul, ornamented by so many virtues, passed back to its Maker. She was buried in Marburg, where a beautiful church has been built in her honor.

THOMAS AQUINAS.

Princeps doctrinæ Scholasti-
cæ

St. Thomas Aquinas, AD 1274

Theodor Berthold

St. Thomas Aquinas was born in the year 1226 in the kingdom of Naples. His father was a count, and was of the family of Aquin. The family home was Castle Rocca-Secca. Even as a child, St. Thomas seemed blessed.

When the boy was five years old he was sent to the Benedictines on Mount Casino for training and instruction. Here he showed as great diligence in study as he did in pious practices. His teachers said that they never before had had such a wonderfully gifted and so touchingly pious a child. Such wonderful gifts of mind as St. Thomas Aquinas had, God has not given every child, but diligent and pious you can all be, and by diligence many natural gifts can be replaced.

Even when he was only ten years old, Thomas had progressed so far in his studies that he could be sent to the high school in Naples. Here he carefully avoided all dangerous society; prayer and study were his preference. He liked, too, to give alms to the poor. Full of love for Jesus and filled with a dislike for worldly pleasures, he decided when he was seventeen years old to enter the Dominican Order.

This resolve was doubtless pleasing to God, but worldly-minded people tried to persuade Thomas not to do so. His mother was against the religious life; his proud brothers, Landulf and Raynald, could not bear to think that a count of Aquin should become a beggarly monk, as they put it. Everything was tried by them to turn Thomas from his desire. And when persuasion did not succeed, they did not hesitate to use force.

To protect Thomas against the persecutions of his relatives, his superiors sent him to Paris. He started out on the journey, but his brothers seized him, dragged him to the family castle, and locked him up in a tower. Here Thomas was a prisoner for two years. But nothing was able to shake his steadfastness, and his determination to heed the voice of God rather than the commands of men.

A woman who was sent into his room to tempt him he drove out with a burning firebrand from the hearth. His two sisters who tried to coax him to give up the religious life were so carried away, when he spoke to them as if inspired of the vanity of earthly things, that they let their brother down from

246

the tower in a basket. Below his brother monks received him.

After returning to the monastery, Thomas was sent to Cologne by his superiors, to attend the lectures of the great Albertus Magnus, whose renown then reached to every part of Europe. Under this great teacher Thomas made wonderful progress. Nevertheless, he was so humble and silent that some of his fellow pupils nicknamed him the "silent ox." But Albertus Magnus said this ox would soon make a sound that the whole world would hear.

When he was barely twenty-two years old, Thomas became a professor. As such he taught in Paris, in Bologna, Fondi, Pisa, and Orvieto with extraordinary success. It was true: the whole world spoke of him and heard of him. He was looked upon as a giant of knowledge. But did he become vain? Oh, no; humbly he once followed to market a lay brother who did not know him, and carried a basket for him. He only sought to promote the glory of God by his knowledge and his angelically pure life. Prayer was his constant companion. Indeed, he attained to his great wisdom chiefly by prayer. The Holy Spirit inspired him when he occupied himself with the mysteries of God.

The saint wrote many books on the truths of the faith, and these are written with such clearness and are thought out so acutely that they are to this day the foundation of the study of theology. When Thomas had completed a part of his works, the Lord said to him: "Thou hast written well of Me, Thomas. What dost thou ask for reward?" To which the saint answered, "Nothing but Thee, Lord."

Exhausted by his great mental labors, Thomas wished to retire to the monastery at Naples, which was very dear to him. But Pope Gregory X sent for him to come to the Council at Lyons. On the way there the saint had an attack of fever. He was received and cared for in the convent of Fossa Nuova, but on the 7th of March, 1274, he went home to God, the First Source of all wisdom.

St. Thomas Aquinas, like St. Augustine and St. Ambrose, is called a doctor of the Church[74], and because he was truly an angel in his labors as a teacher, he is called the "angelic doctor."

---

74   By Roman Catholic Christians.

St. Catherine of Siena, AD 1380

Amy Steedman

As the years pass by time makes many changes in the busy town and quiet country, but there are some places he seems to have forgotten or passed over so lightly that they look very much the same today as they did hundreds of years ago.

One of these places, which time has dealt so gently with, is in the heart of Italy, built high upon a hill. It is a town whose towers and palaces and steep, narrow streets are little changed from what they were six hundred and more years ago, when Catherine, the saint of Siena, was born there.

Today if you climb the steep winding road that leads up to the city and make your way through the gates and along the steepest of the narrow streets, you will come to a house with a motto written over the door in golden letters— "Sposæ Christi Katharinæ domus," which means "The house of Katherine, the bride of Christ." And if you go in you will see the very room

where Saint Catherine used to live, the bed of planks on which she slept, her little chapel, and the rooms which her brothers and sisters used.

It all looks just as it did when Benincasa, the dyer of Siena, lived there with his wife Lapa. They had more than twenty children, but each one was welcome, and when at last Catherine and a twin sister were born, there still did not seem one too many. The little sister lived only a few days, and perhaps that made the parents love Catherine all the more, and it was not only her own family who loved her. She was the favorite of all the neighbors, and however busy they were they would always find time to stop and talk to her as they passed. It was not that she was very beautiful, or even very clever, but she had a way of making everyone feel happy when she was near them, and she had the sunniest smile that ever dimpled a baby's face. It was like a sunbeam, lighting up everything near it, and it shone in her eyes as well, so that ere long the people found a new name for her, and called her "Joy" instead of Catherine.

As soon as she could walk alone, Catherine would wander away, sure of a welcome at every house, and though at first when the other children cried, "The baby is lost again!" the mother would be anxious, she soon ceased to mind, and only said, "She is sure to be safe somewhere."

And safe she always was, for everyone would stop work to look after her as she toddled along, and wherever she went Joy carried the sunshine with her.

It happened that one afternoon when Catherine was about six years old, her mother sent her and an elder brother, Stephen, to carry a message to a house some way off. It was a beautiful evening, and as the children went hand in hand down the steep street and up the hill towards the great church of Saint Dominic, Catherine stopped a moment to look at the sunset. She always loved beautiful colors, and tonight the little fleecy clouds were all touched with crimson and gold, like fairy islands in a pale green sea, more beautiful than anything she had ever seen.

Stephen did not care for sunsets. He was much more anxious to be home in time for supper, so he ran on alone, calling to Catherine to follow quickly.

Catherine did not seem to hear his voice or to notice that he was gone, but stood there with eyes fixed on the sunset, her face shining, and her hair like a halo of gold round her head.

It was not the evening sky she was looking at, but a vision of heavenly beauty. For there among the rose-pink clouds she saw the Madonna seated upon a throne and holding in her arms the infant Christ, her dazzling robe blue as the summer sky, and a jeweled crown upon her head. Only the same sweet mother-look was there as when she bent over the manger-bed. There are no words to tell of the beauty of the Christ-child's face. Catherine only knew that as He looked at her, He smiled and held up His little hand as if in blessing, and that smile drew her heart to His feet.

Then suddenly Catherine's arm was roughly shaken, and her brother asked her impatiently at what she was gazing.

"O Stephen," she cried, "did you not see it too? Look!"

But the vision had faded, and the grey twilight closed in upon the two little figures as they went slowly home, the boy vexed with his loitering sister, and she sobbing with disappointment to think that the window in heaven was shut, and that she might never again look within.

As Catherine grew older, she never forgot the vision she had seen, or how the hand of the Christ-child had been stretched out to bless her. And it made her think often how she could best please Him, so that someday He might smile on her again.

Catherine had heard a great deal about the good men who went to live in deserts to be alone with God,—how they lived in caves and had scarcely anything to eat, and how God would sometimes send the ravens to bring them food.[75] Now she was always fond of wandering, and the idea of living in a desert seemed a beautiful way of serving Christ. She had never gone

---

75   1 Kings 17:2-6

beyond the walls of the town, and all outside was a new world to her; so she was sure if only she could pass through the city gates, she would soon find her way to the desert, where there would certainly be a cave ready for her to live in.

So one day Catherine set out very early in the morning, carrying in her pocket a small loaf of bread, just in case the ravens should forget to come to a little girl-hermit.

In those days it was not safe to live outside the city walls, and there were no farms nor houses to be seen as Catherine slipped through the gates and began to find her way down the hillside, among tangled briars and over rough stones. Soon her feet grew very tired, and everything looked so forlorn and wild that she was sure this must be the desert at last, and there, too, was a little cave in the rocks waiting all ready for her.

It was very nice to creep in and out of the hot sunshine into the cool shade, and to rest until the sun went down. But as night came on and she knelt to say her evening prayer, she began to think of home, and the kind mother waiting there, and she knew she had done wrong to come away, even though she had meant to serve God.

Very quickly she left her cave, and as she ran home her feet seemed to fly over the ground. The desert had not been so very far away after all, and she reached the house before her mother had begun to grow anxious, but she never again wandered away to live a hermit's life.

As Catherine grew older, she loved to listen to the stories of the saints, and there was one she was never tired of hearing. It was the life of Saint Catherine of Alexandria, the saint whose name she bore.

This young queen was said to be the wisest and noblest of all the saints, and when her courtiers wished her to marry, she said she would only marry a prince who was perfect in every way. Such a prince was of course impossible to find. The more Catherine thought about this story the more she longed that Christ would accept her heart and service too. And one night in a dream He seemed to come to her, placing a ring upon her finger, and bidding her remember that now she had given her heart to Him.

Thus it was a great trouble to Catherine when she was told by her parents soon after this that she was old enough to begin to think of marriage. She said she did not wish to marry at all. But this only made her parents angry with her, especially when one day they found she had cut off all her beautiful golden hair, thinking to make herself so ugly that no one would want her for his wife.

"Very well," said her father, "if thou wilt not marry as I bid thee, then shalt thou do the house-work and be our servant."

He expected this would be a great punishment, but Catherine was glad to have hard work to do and did it so well and cheerfully that her father began to feel his anger melt away. Then it happened one day that in passing her room he looked in, and there he saw her kneeling with clasped hands and upturned face, and eyes in which the peace of heaven shone, while around her head was a bright light that took the form of a snow-white dove resting there.

From that moment he ceased to be angry with Catherine, and said all should be as she wished, for surely the dove was a sign that God accepted her prayers and approved of what she did.

So she was allowed to have a little room which she made into a chapel where she could be alone to think and to pray. She wanted to learn to conquer herself before she could serve Christ in the world, and for three years she lived almost entirely alone, praying in the little chapel, struggling to overcome her faults and to grow strong to resist temptation.

But in spite of all her struggles evil thoughts would come into her heart, and it seemed impossible to keep them out. It was easy to do right things, but so terribly difficult to think only pure and good thoughts. She knew that Satan sent the wicked thoughts into her heart, but the hardest trial of all was that Christ seemed to have left her to fight alone—He seemed so very far away.

At last one night, as she lay sobbing in despair, suddenly the evil thoughts left her, and instead she felt that Christ was near and that He bent tenderly over her.

"Why, oh why didst Thou leave me so long, dear Lord?" she cried.

"I never left thee," His voice said quietly.

"But where were Thou, Lord, when all was so dark and evil?" she humbly asked.

"I was in thy heart," replied the voice; "didst thou not hate the evil thoughts? If I had not been there, thou wouldst not have felt how black they were, but because I was in the midst they seemed to thee most evil, and thus I gave thee strength to cast them out."

So Catherine's heart was filled with peace, and she learned to love Christ more and more, and to deny herself in every way, sleeping on bare planks with a log for her pillow, and eating the things she cared for least.

It was not that she thought these things good in themselves, but she felt she must use every means to make her heart pure and fit to serve her Master.

And before very long Christ spoke to her again in the stillness of the night, and told her she had lived long enough alone, that it was time now to go out into the world and help other people to grow good too.

When Catherine thought of the busy, noisy life which other people led, compared to the quiet peacefulness of her little cell and chapel, she was very sad, and thought she had offended God that He was sending her away from Him to mix with the world again. But His voice sounded in her ears once more and told her it was not to separate her from Himself that He sent her out, but that she should learn to help others.

"Thou knowest that love giveth two commandments—to love Me, and to love thy neighbor. I desire that thou shouldst walk not on one but two feet, and fly to heaven on two wings."

So Christ spoke to her, and Catherine with fearful heart prepared to obey, only praying that He would give her strength to do His will. And after that her life was spent in doing good to others.

The smile that used to lighten her face when she was a little child had still the power of bringing peace and gladness to all, as she went amongst the poor, nursing the sick, helping everyone in trouble, and teaching people more by her life than her words to love God.

And as, when she was a baby, they called her Joy, so now again they found a new name for her, and she was known as "the child of the people." In every kind of trouble they came to her, even asking her to settle their quarrels, so that she was the peacemaker as well as the helper of the whole town.

There was one special reason why people loved Catherine, and that was because she always saw the best that was in them. She knew there was good in everyone, no matter how it was dimmed or hidden by the evil that wrapped it round. Where other eyes saw only evil temper or wicked spite, she looked beyond until she found some good that she could love. Every day she prayed to God that He would help her to see the beauty in each soul, so that she might help it to get rid of the sin that dimmed its beauty. And so, because she looked for good in everyone, all showed her what was best in themselves, and for very shame would strive to be all that she thought them.

Catherine had joined the Dominican sisterhood and wore the white robe and black veil, but she did not live in a convent as other sisters did. Every morning when the sun began to gild the towers and roofs of the city, passers-by would see her leave her home and walk up the steep street towards the church of Saint Dominic where she always went to early mass.

Strangers must have wondered when they saw the men uncover their heads as she passed, as if she had been a queen instead of a poor sister clad in a coarse white robe and black veil. But if they had caught sight of her face perhaps, they would have understood, for her eyes seemed as if they were looking into heaven, and the holy peace that shone in her smile made men feel that she lived in the very presence of God.

One morning as she was going to church as usual in the first light of dawn, her thoughts far away and her lips moving in prayer, she was startled by the touch of a hand upon her robe and the sound of a voice asking for help. She turned to look and saw a poor man leaning against the wall, haggard and pale, and so weak that he could scarcely stand.

"What dost thou want of me?" asked Catherine pitifully.

"I only ask a little help for my journey," the poor man said; "my home is far from here, and the fever laid its hand upon me as I worked to provide bread for those I love. So I pray thee, lady, give me a little money that I may buy food to strengthen me before I start."

"I would gladly help thee," answered Catherine most sorrowfully, "but I am not a lady, only a poor sister, and I have no money of my own to give."

She turned as if to go on, but the eager hand still held her cloak and the man begged once more.

"For Christ's sake help me, for indeed I need thy help most sorely."

Then Catherine stood still. She felt she could not leave him so. There was nothing at home she could part with, for that very morning she had given away all the food that was in the house. Her father and mother were good and kind, but she must not give away the things they needed. Sorrowful and perplexed, her hand felt for the rosary which hung at her side, for in every trouble she ever turned in prayer to her dear Lord. Then as her fingers touched the beads, she suddenly remembered that here was at least one thing which was her very own—a small silver cross which she had had since she was a child, and which she had touched so often as she prayed that it was worn smooth and thin.

Still it was silver and would buy the sick man a meal, and she quickly unfastened it from the rosary and put it into his hand. The man's blessings followed her as she went, and though she had parted with the thing she loved best, she counted the blessings more precious than the gift.

And as she knelt in the dim church, after the mass was over, God sent a heavenly vision to reward His servant.

Catherine thought she stood in a great hall filled with things more beautiful than words can tell, and in the midst stood our Blessed Lord, holding in His hand the most beautiful thing of all—a cross of beaten gold, set with jewels of every hue sparkling so brightly that it almost dazzled Catherine's eyes as she looked.

"Dost thou see these shining gifts," He asked, "and wouldst thou know whence they came? They are the noble deeds which men have done for My sake."

And Catherine kneeling there with her empty hands could

only bow her head and say: "Lord, I am only a poor sister, as Thou knowest, and have nought to give Thee. The service I can offer could not find a place among these glorious gifts."

Then it seemed as if Christ smiled upon her, and holding out the golden cross He asked: "Hast thou not seen this cross before, Catherine?"

"No, Lord," she answered, wondering, "never before have mine eyes beheld anything so lovely."

But as she gazed upon it, her heart was filled with a sudden gladness, for in the midst of the gold and jewels, in the heart of the glorious light, she saw the little worn silver cross which she had given to the poor man that morning for the love of Christ.

And as the vision faded there rang in her ears the words she knew so well: "Inasmuch as ye did it unto one of the least of these My brethren, ye did it unto Me."[76]

As time went on the fame of Catherine spread to other towns, outside Siena, and when there were disputes between the great cities of Italy they would send for Catherine, and beg her to act as peacemaker, and she helped them all just as she did her own poor people of Siena. Even the Pope came to her for advice.

In the midst of all this busy life Catherine fell ill. Her love for Christ was so real, and her sorrow for His sufferings so

---

76   Matthew 25:40

great, that she prayed that she might bear the pain that He had borne. All her sufferings she bore most patiently, but her heart was glad when the end came.

The same vision that had smiled on her that summer evening when she was a child, appeared in the sunset sky again, this time never to fade away, as Catherine, the bride of Christ, was led by the white-robed angels up to the throne of our Lord.

Philippoteaux, del.

Roze, sc.

JEANNE D'ARC.

Blessée au Siège de Paris

St. Jeanne d'Arc, AD 1431

Lena Dalkeith

Most of which is taken from the *Ancient Chronicles*
written down at her trial and afterwards.

This right marvelous and true tale begins in the year of Our
Lord 1424, when Jeanne was but thirteen years old.

A fine, tall maid was she, strong and shapely in body, fair of
face, sweet and gentle in manner, but of a keen wit and humor
withal. She lived in the little village of Domremy, which stood
then outside the fair Kingdom of France, close on the borders
of the Duchy of Burgundy.

The good folks of Domremy, however, were all for France.
They hated and despised the Burgundians because the Burgundians sided with the English against France, and everyone
knows how at that time the French feared and hated the English
more than any in the world.

And they had good cause for their fear, I warrant you. For
many a black year the English army had wandered over France,
fighting capturing, and pillaging wherever they went, and never

losing a battle. So that at last the French had lost courage. It seemed to them that, however well they fought, the English had the best of it.

Besides, the French had no real, true crowned King of their own to lead them. Some years before Jeanne was born, an English King had married a French Princess. Some of the French nobles had foolishly promised that if a son should be born of the marriage, he should inherit the throne of France. Now in this they did great wrong, sinning in loyalty against Charles the Dauphin, son of their dead King.

He, the true heir to the throne, must therefore wander from town to town through France with a few courtiers, fleeing the English or fighting them, as best seemed fit; and not only was he in danger from the English who had vowed to conquer France, but also from the Burgundians, who were their allies.

Moreover, this poor prince had scarce money enough to pay his bootmaker, and worse trouble than all, there were many even among his own Court who doubted if he were in truth the real son of the King. Even his own mother, who sided with the Burgundians, would speak no word in his favor, so that Charles, doubtful himself and very miserable, sometimes wondered if he had not better give up all hope and flee to Spain, leaving France in the hands of the English.

One day he went apart by himself and sorrowfully prayed

to God in his heart (speaking no word of the prayer aloud, mark you), to let him know by some clear sign whether he had a royal right to the throne of France or whether he had none.

And now, hear ye awhile of the Blessed Maid who was to save France from the hands of her enemies. As has already been made known to you, the story begins in her thirteenth year, when she first heard the commands of God spoken through the voice of the Archangel Michael.

It happened in summer, while she walked in her father's garden. It was noontide and very warm. As she walked, Jeanne thought of many things—of the race she had won running with her comrades that day, of the poor soldier who had come back from the war sore wounded and sorrowful. Jeanne, little maid as she was, felt a great pity in her heart for the fair land of France. She longed to do something to help. On a sudden, before her, upon the right side, between her and the church, she saw a bright and radiant light, which dazzled her eyes so they were blinded for a space. Presently when she had become more used to the light and dared to look again, she saw an angel's face appearing through the wondershine, and heard a voice which said: "Jeanne, the Lord God hath chosen thee to save France."

"Alas!" cried the maid, "how may I save our beautiful France who am but a poor village girl who tends sheep? How can such as I lead forth soldiers to war?"

"Be a good girl," said the angel; and again, "Be a good girl, little Jeanne," and then he went away.

Now you may believe this or not as you will, everyone has a right to his own opinion; nevertheless, this story is true. Strange, marvelous as it may appear, Jeanne's word has been proved true a hundred times over, despite all her enemies could do; and this that I have told you is almost word for word what she told her cruel judges about the first coming of the angels.

Jeanne wept when the light vanished, and she heard the voice no more. But after that she tried harder than ever to be good. And the light came again and other angels, St. Catherine and St. Margaret, whom she loved above all the saints. Sometimes she saw them and touched them, but more often she heard them speak, and ever the words they spoke were to the same end. "Jeanne, be good, and thou shalt save France."

To herself Jeanne called them "My Voices," or "My Counsel," but to her father and friends in Domremy she breathed never a word of what had happened her until later.

Meanwhile matters grew worse in France, and when Jeanne was scarcely seventeen years old the voices became more urgent. They began to tell her what to do. "Go into France, Jeanne," they said; "it is time."

And one day they told her that she must rescue the town of Orleans, for it was in great danger. Orleans was the only town in France which remained true to the Dauphin; if the Dauphin lost it, he lost all France with it.

Then the voices told Jeanne how she was to reach Orleans, and she obeyed them in all things. This is what she did. She left her father and her mother and her home—remember it was by God's command that she went, and He gave her strength and courage to do it. She left Domremy and journeyed to Vaucouleurs, a strong embattled town loyal to France and not far from Domremy.

There she went straight to Robert de Baudricourt, the captain of the town, and told her story, how by the command of God she was come to save France. Baudricourt, as you may believe, laughed at her, refusing to believe a word she said.

"A foolish, dreaming girl," he said; "turn her away."

But she came again to him, saying earnestly, "Today the gentle Dauphin hath great hurt from the town of Orleans, and yet greater will he have if you do not send me to him."

Now, the day on which Jeanne told the captain this was the twelfth of February, she being informed by her voices; and on the twelfth of February the Dauphin was defeated with great loss by the English at the battle of Rouvray.

A few days later, for tidings came but slowly in olden times, news was brought to Baudricourt of the battle and of the Dauphin's loss. Baudricourt, remembering Jeanne's words, and wondering greatly, began to believe in this strange maid and her high mission. He told her he was ready to do what she asked of him.

Obeying the voices, she begged for a grey doublet, black hose, and horse, and an escort. So, clad like a boy, riding upon a great horse and accompanied by a knight, a squire, and four men-at-arms, Jeanne set out for Chinon, where the Dauphin then was.

They rode far and fast and at last came to Chinon, where Jeanne was lodged with a kindly dame who took good care of her. Already word of her coming and of her strange daring and confidence had gone forth over the land. Yet most men scoffed, crying: "How shall a slight girl stand up against these terrible English?"

On the second day after Jeanne's coming to Chinon, the Prince received her in spite of all his courtiers could say to prevent him. These nobles of his court were afraid lest the girl might unsettle the Prince and so disturb their pleasure. Not one believed there was a word of truth in her story.

When the maid was brought into the hall of the castle where the King had his court, she beheld a crowd of gallant-looking men and women clad in rich and splendid dress. Before she came in, the Dauphin had given his mantle to a courtier in exchange for a simple cloak, and he stood among his nobles as one of them.

Everyone expected the maid to fall on her knees before the courtier, who wore the King's gorgeous mantle. Jeanne did no such thing. Paying no heed to anyone, nay, looking at no one but the true Dauphin, she went straight to him and, kneeling, said:

"This is the fair Prince to whom I am sent."

"Nay, I am not the Dauphin," answered the Prince, wishing to try her further.

"If you are not he," answered Jeanne, "then my voices have betrayed me, and that could not be. My voices have shown me that you are the Prince whose kingdom I must save, and whom I shall crown at Rheims before the year be out."

"Ah me, if that might be!" Charles said wistfully.

"It shall be," answered the maid. "Give me an audience alone for a few moments, gentle Dauphin, and you shall believe me."

Wondering at this strange girl, the Dauphin later spoke with her alone, and what she told him he told a friend long afterwards, when he was old. Jeanne herself would never tell what passed between them, not even when they tortured her on her trial. It was the Dauphin's secret, and she kept it faithfully.

We, who have read what the Dauphin said, know that Jeanne told him that God had answered his secret, silent prayer, and sent her to assure him that he was the true and rightful heir to the throne of France, the eldest son of the dead King, the prince whom she had been sent to crown.

What could Charles do but believe this holy, heaven-sent maid? Nevertheless, to make quite sure, he sent her to Poitiers, there to be questioned and examined by wise bishops and priests. These clever men did their best to find out all about Jeanne. They questioned and they questioned, and not one single false word could they accuse the maid of having spoken. Her answers were often so simple, so witty, so wise, that they marveled daily. All their questioning and Jeanne's answers were written down in a book, and they can be read unto this day.

In six weeks they sent Jeanne back to the King, and this was their judgment: "The maid is good and true. Believe in her."

After this, Charles began to do more what Jeanne told him to do. He set about gathering together an army for her; he had white armor made for her (for she always wore the dress of a boy until the day of her death), and a shield and a banner.

When he would have given her a sword, she refused, bidding them send to a certain chapel named after St. Catherine, in which she said the sword lay buried which was for her use. When they obeyed her, sure enough, they found an old rusty sword there, with five crosses upon it. This she wore always, but used rarely even in battle, so gentle was she, so much did she dislike to take away life.

The French soldiers were all very eager to follow this new and strange girl-captain. She roused all the courage there was in them, for they believed that she and she only could lead them triumphantly against the English. But although the whole army loved her, and she it, Jeanne was a very strict, stern captain. She would allow no feasting, no drinking, no swearing, even among her generals.

When the soldiers were all ready, Jeanne, obeying her voices, led them straight to Orleans, which was by this time in very great danger from the English.

On the 29th of April 1422, the French army had passed the enemy's lines and entered Orleans. Perhaps dates of battles are not very interesting things to you, but mark you this, if you would understand something of the glory of the maid. As a general no one could match her, and as for her skill in using cannon, no one could surpass it.

The French reached Orleans on the 29th of April, upon a Friday. Upon the Wednesday afterwards, that is, upon the 4th of May, Jeanne led out her men and took one of the English forts called St. Loup.

Upon the second day after that she took the fort of St. Augustine, and on the next Sunday she fought again, and so fiercely, that the English retired in dismay. Orleans, after its long siege, was saved.

The English were not only vexed at being defeated, but they were sore ashamed that the victory had been won by a woman. "She must be a witch," the soldiers said; and at the thought of fighting a witch the courage of even the bravest of them failed.

It had been easy for them to fight the French before this, because the French had been so often defeated that they did not fight well; but now with their beloved maid to lead them in her shining armor, they were foes of very different metal.

Orleans now safe, Jeanne wanted to take the Dauphin to Rheims and crown him. No King of France was thought to be a real king until he had been crowned at Rheims and anointed with the Holy Oil that was kept there for that purpose.

But to reach Rheims many towns had to be recaptured from the English, and the Dauphin was not over anxious to go. Now from the beginning the voices had warned Jeanne that she had only a year's time in which to do all that she had to do; and that year dated from May 1429. This she told the Dauphin over and over again, hoping to rouse him to come with her to Rheims.

But the Dauphin was surrounded by lazy courtiers who did not want to move, being very comfortable where they were, and all the Dauphin did was to summon Council after Council to consider what should be done. Jeanne grew tired of waiting.

"I have four things to do," she said. "To drive the English in flight from our country, to deliver the Duke of Orleans who is their prisoner, to crown the King at Rheims, and to raise the siege of Orleans. This last is done. Now must we fight our way to Rheims."

The Dauphin had made her waste one month of her precious year. So she set out without him and defeated the famous English general, Talbot, at Pathay, on an open battlefield. Even then it was hard to make the Dauphin move; even though Jeanne told him that all the cities, instead of fighting, would open their gates to him.

When at last he did begin the march, Charles found the Maid's words were true. With little or no trouble he came to Rheims, to the great joy of all France.

On the 17th of July, Jeanne with a great and fair company of noble knights brought the King along the streets of Rheims to the beautiful Cathedral. He entered with much pomp and splendor to the sound of singing, and then with much rejoicing the Archbishop anointed and crowned the Dauphin King of France.

Jeanne, as she knelt to do the King homage and swear the oath of fealty, wept for very joy. Two of her high tasks were done. Soon she would perform the rest and be free at last to go back to her own little village and see her father and mother again. That was what she longed to do more than anything else in the world, but first her duty must be done.

King Charles now asked her what reward he could give her, to which she answered: "Fair King, I would that the people of my village should be freed from the paying of taxes for three hundred years;" and the King said, "So it shall be," and he caused to be written on the books of the accounts of the villages after the name of Domremy and of the village next to it:

"Nothing, for the sake of the Maid."

As they rode from the Cathedral, the Archbishop asked Jeanne if she feared anything.

"Nought but treachery," she answered.

Alas and alas! how shall I tell of the treachery that worked against her ever after that glorious day at Rheims?

Unwitting of it, she rode to Paris, which was in the hands of the Burgundians, the allies of the English.

"We must take Paris," quoth she, "and when Paris is ours, all France will be ours, and I shall go home to Domremy and be happy again." Jeanne's words would have come true had she been allowed her own way, but she was not.

The weak Dauphin let his lazy favorites persuade him to do as they wanted, so that instead of hurrying to help the Maid lay siege to Paris, he loitered with his army at this town or that on the way, and when he at last came to Paris, it was too late, for the English had brought up an army to help their allies.

Jeanne, meanwhile, had been attacking the walls bravely and had done good work. Every day she led out her men, and from dawn to night-time they fought in the trenches. It was wonderful to hear the noise of the guns and culverins[77] from the walls.

When Charles with his soldiers at last showed themselves, the Maid was full confident they could storm the city. But she relied on the King's army to help, and again the King failed her, for hearing that she was wounded, he sent word of command to her to stop the fighting.

Very, very reluctantly, and sad at heart, she obeyed. The next day, however, she and her friend, the Duke of Alencon, who has told us many of her doings, made ready again to fight, for Jeanne's wound was slight. Again came word from the King forbidding them to begin. More than that, he ordered a bridge to be destroyed which Jeanne had caused to be built, so that she could cross the river Seine the very next day and attack Paris from another quarter.

You can picture to yourself how disappointed Jeanne and her eager soldiers were; their plans spoilt, their hopes of victory crushed by this timid King, whose word they must obey. And

---

77 A primitive form of cannon.

worse was to come; for Charles, hoodwinked by evil counsellors and anxious for peace, would not let Jeanne fight again for six long months.

The Maid's heart nigh broke, and all her generals and soldiers mourned with her. So they waited while the foolish King tried to make peace with the Duke of Burgundy, who was only the Governor of Paris because the English wanted him to be.

So the year 1429, which might have meant so much more to France had the Maid been let alone to do as she willed, passed away, and the next year, 1430, wore on to spring. You will remember that Jeanne's year finished in May 1430. The time was very near. The voices which had all the time spoken and counselled Jeanne in all that she did, now spoke to her again, but they gave her little cheer.

"It needs must be that you shall be taken prisoner before Midsummer Day," said they. "But do thou be of good cheer and God will send you help."

Jeanne's heart sank within her and she grew afraid. She prayed to God that she might die in battle rather than be taken prisoner. She knew too well that the English would tie her to a stake and burn her to death if they once could capture her; for the English firmly believed she was a witch, and it was the custom to burn witches in those days.

Nevertheless, in spite of her great fear, in spite of hearing the same dreadful words from the voices over and over again, Jeanne went out to fight when she could, as bravely as of old; and of the many brave and noble deeds this is thought to be the bravest and the noblest thing she did, for she went out to fight in a very different way from before.

Before this, the voices had warned her of danger, had told her what to do, and had guided her to victory. Now they were silent; they let her act as she would, and they never told her the day or the hour when she was to be captured.

And so Jeanne, instead of taking the lead, took the advice of her captains and generals. It was the best she could do, for she was never sure of victory, as had always been before.

One day news came that the good city of Compiegne, which was loyal to France, had been laid siege to by a great army of English and Burgundians. Jeanne, who loved that city, at once set out to its rescue, and with only a few hundred men in her company she rode into the town under cover of night.

The people received her with great joy, for wherever Jeanne went she brought hope and joy. This was on the dawn of the 23rd day of May 1430. At five o'clock in the morning she led out her men to the attack, hoping to surprise the enemy. So she did, driving them back twice; and then (alas! that this must be told) up came the main body of the enemy to help the Burgundians. They forced Jeanne to fall back towards the city. Before she and her little troop could reach the gates, up rushed the English between her and the bridge that leads into Compiegne.

The fear in Jeanne's heart grew. Bravely she spurred her horse up the raised causeway, and leaped into the meadow below. There she was at once surrounded by the Burgundians, who called her to surrender. "Never!" she cried, hoping they would kill her on the spot. But this they were not likely to do, for Jeanne was worth a large sum of money to her captors. Either King Charles would ransom her, or they could sell her to the English, who would give much to get this Maid into their hands.

And now you must hear of Jeanne's troubles even to their cruel end. This gentlest, noblest, bravest maid that ever lived in all the world was sold to the English. The King of France, whom she had crowned, made no effort to save her. The English bought her and, having done so, gave her into the hands of the French priests, who were on their side, so she might be tried by them for being a witch and a heretic, a worker of magic, and many other horrible things, none of which were true.

She was brought to her trial at Rouen, where no mercy was ever shown to her by her enemies. The greatest of these was Cauchon, Bishop of Beauvais. Someday, when you are old enough, you can read if you will the whole account of the trial, which was written down at that time, and has since been translated into English.

You will see how bravely the Maid stood up against an army of bishops, priests, and lawyers, all questioning her, all waiting to find fault with her answers and make them out to be lies. You will read how they tortured her to try and make her confess that her voices were the voices of devils, and not of angels.

They could do nothing with her. She told her story simply and truthfully, and the voices helped her many a time to outwit her captors. Yet there came a time even when they seemed to have left her and she stood alone. Once in her darkest hour she denied having heard the voices, but very quickly she repented and never lost courage again.

Always they tormented her over the boy's dress she wore by command of the voices, and it was the wearing of the boy's dress which gave those cruel and malicious priests the excuse for condemning her to death.

They said that she committed a sin against God by so doing, and yet would give her no chance to change, and by a cruel act of treachery they condemned her to death.

In the marketplace at Rouen they burned her to death at the stake upon May the 24th, 1431. One whole year had she lain in prison for her trial, and she was only nineteen years old when she died.

They put eight hundred soldiers around the stake for fear

anyone should try to save her, and on her brow they set a paper cap, on which was written, "Heretic, Relapsed, Apostate, Idolatress."

Lightly the true Maid went to her cruel death, and gladly she died, bowing her head and calling on the name of Jesus, and the English threw her ashes into the sea so men should forget her. How could they think men should forget such a maid? The whole world owes her reverence now, for no more beautiful spirit ever lived on earth.

In the town of Orleans now every eighth of May they hold a feast in her honor, while many a town has its statue of her. Her fair name has been cleared, for some time after her death there was another trial. Everyone who knew her came to testify to her truth and goodness, so that even in her own age men had some dim idea of doing justice to her memory.

As for the English after their cruel burning of Jeanne, nothing prospered with them in France. They were driven back again to England, with no least chance of ever winning again the Crown which by right belonged to the Kings of France.

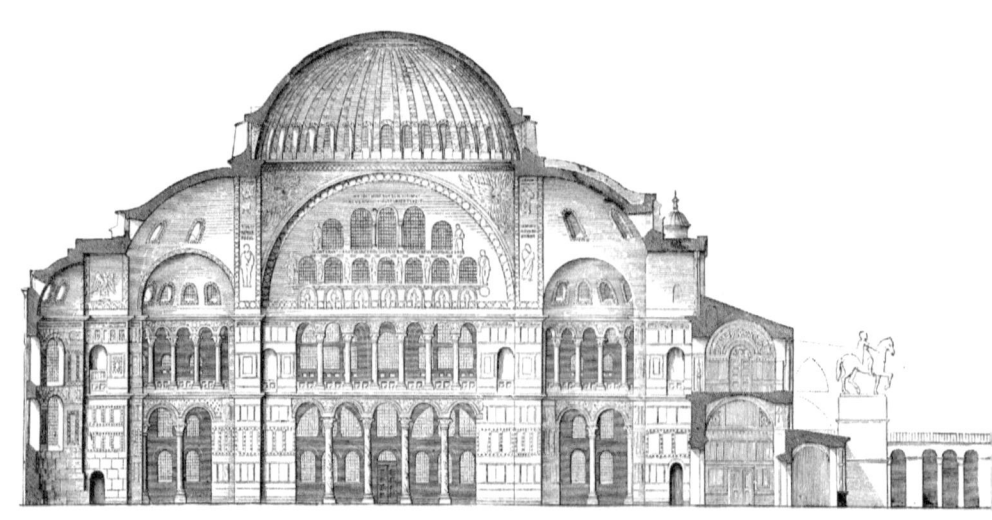

The Fall of
Constantinople,
AD 1453

Eva March Tappan

The country of Turkey had been part of the Eastern Empire
even after the fall of Rome in 476, but it had come to be so
little Roman and so completely Greek that it is spoken of as
the Greek, or Byzantine, Empire. It was destined, however, to
belong to neither Romans nor Greeks, for the Mohammedans
were pressing hard upon its boundaries. They had won Asia
Minor and the lands lying directly south of the Danube. Gradually they got Greece, north of the Isthmus, into their power,
and in 1453 Mohammed II led the Ottoman Turks, who were of
the same race as Attila and his Huns, against the capital of the
Eastern Empire, the great rich city of Constantinople.

Gunpowder had been invented before this time, but the
cannon were small. When the great Turkish gun fired its heavy
stone balls, men and women rushed into the streets, beating
their breasts and crying aloud, "God have mercy upon us!" Day

after day the besiegers continued the attack. They used arrows, catapults for throwing stones, and a few rifles. They wheeled a two-story tower covered with buffalo hides near enough to the city so that archers in the second story could shoot at the defenders on the walls. But the Greeks threw their famous Greek fire upon it and it burned to ashes. Both parties dug mines. Sometimes these were blown up, sometimes the workers in them were suffocated by smoke or gas.

Finally the Turks dug a narrow canal five miles long from the Sea of Marmora to the harbor of Constantinople. They paved it with beams, well-greased, and one morning the Greeks found thirty Turkish ships lying almost under their walls, for the buffaloes of the Turks had dragged them to the shore during the night. Then the people of the city were in despair and begged their emperor to escape and flee for his life, but he refused. "I am resolved to die here with you," he declared.

When it was seen that the city must fall, thousands of the citizens crowded into the vast church of St. Sophia, for there was an old prophecy that someday the Turks would force their way into the city, but that when they had reached St. Sophia an angel would appear with a celestial sword, and that at sight of it the Turks would flee. The emperor knelt long in prayer, received the Holy Communion, and then begged the priests and all the members of his court to forgive him if he had ever wronged them. The sobs and wails of the people echoed in the great building.

The Turks made their way without hindrance into the city. They did not stop at the church; and no angel brought a miraculous weapon to drive them back. The emperor fell, sword in hand, fighting to the last for his empire and the Christian faith. The Turkish commander gave over the city to his soldiers, and they stole everything worth stealing,—wonderful treasures of gold, silver, bronze, and jewels. Thousands of citizens were roughly bound together and dragged off to the boats to be sold as slaves. The cross was torn down from beautiful St. Sophia, and the crescent, the emblem of Mohammedanism, was put in its place.

The emperor's body, however, was buried by the Turks with all honors. A lamp was lighted at his grave. It is still kept burning, and at the charge of the Turkish government. This was commanded by the Turkish ruler as a mark of respect and regard for Constantine Palaologos, the last Christian emperor in the Empire of the East.

At the coming of the Turks, many of the Greeks had seized their most valued treasures and fled. The scholars carried away with them the rare old manuscripts of the early Greek writers. More went to Italy than anywhere else, and the Italian scholars gave them a hearty welcome. There had been learned Greeks in Italy long before this time, and the Italian scholars had been interested in the Greek literature; but now such a wealth of it was poured into the country that the Italians were aroused and delighted. They read the manuscripts eagerly; they sent copies to their friends; and gradually a knowledge of the literature of the Greeks and a love for it spread throughout Europe.

MARTIN LUTHER, AD 1546

M.B. SYNGE

Erasmus was sixteen years old when Martin Luther was born, —Martin Luther, the great German Reformer, whose name was soon to be known throughout the whole continent of Europe. This is the story of his life. He was born in the year 1483. His father was a humble miner, his mother was noted for her goodness and virtue. When quite a little child, his parents wished to make a "scholar" of him—so he was early taught to read and write, and at six years old he was sent to school.

And now a strange thing happened, that altered his whole life. One day he was walking with a friend, when a tremendous thunderstorm came on. A sudden vivid flash of lightning struck near him, making Martin fall the ground. Struck to the heart, he made up his mind that henceforth he would devote his life to God and God's service. In spite of his father's protests he became a monk. For the first two years his life was a very hard

one: his food was very scanty, he had to perform the lowliest tasks, and to beg for alms and bread. Whatever spare time he had, he worked hard at his books, studying the epistles and gospels diligently. In the library of the university he found a complete Bible in Latin. It was the first time he had seen one. He devoured it eagerly. A new light came into his life, and in his close study of the Bible he strengthened himself for his future work. Before long he had risen to a position of importance in the monastery. He became a priest and went to live at Wittenberg—a town which he made famous by his name. In 1509 he began to lecture on the Scriptures. Bibles were not in the hands of all as they are today, and Martin Luther was able to tell his countrymen a great deal that they did not know, by reason of his deep learning. His lectures made a great impression.

"This monk," said the head of the university, "will bring in a new doctrine."

He also began now to preach in the churches. He was very earnest, and the people who listened to him were deeply moved at his words.

In 1511 he was sent on a mission to Rome, where Leo X was Pope. Now, from early times there has been a Pope or Father of Rome, who in the Middle Ages had come to be looked on as the Head of the Christian Church by many, if not all, of the countries of Europe.

Now during the Middle Ages many abuses had crept into the Church. One of these was known as the "sale of indulgences."

All feel it right that sinners should suffer for their sins, but there is no Biblical foundation for the teaching that by money payments a sinner may be saved from the punishment of his sin. Yet, in those days, persons who paid money received an "indulgence," and agents went about the country selling them.

One of these, named John Tetzel, came to Germany. He disgusted Martin Luther by his method of extorting money from ignorant people, and being a man of great courage, Luther felt it his duty to remonstrate[78]. He stood up boldly in his pulpit and denounced the system openly. It was a tremendous moment. It was indeed the visible beginning of the Reformation—that great movement which was to spread wider and wider until it should affect the whole Christian world.

Tetzel was coming to Wittenberg in the autumn of 1517 when Luther determined on more open opposition. It was the eve of All Saints when he posted up on the door of the church ninety-five reasons against the sale of indulgences. He had no idea what a storm he was raising. He did not wish to quarrel with the Pope, only to expose this abuse in the Church. But he had kindled the spark that fired the great Reformation. Wide-

---

78   To forcefully protest.

spread excitement followed, and at last Luther was summoned to Rome to answer for his ninety-five reasons. But the distance was great, and it was agreed that he should go to Augsburg, where a representative of the Pope would meet him.

Martin Luther was but a poor friar still, and he walked the distance, clad in his brown frock with his few wants on his back. His fellow-citizens attended him to the gates and followed him some way along the road.

"Luther forever!" they cried as they bade him farewell.

"No," he answered quietly, "Christ forever!"

Arrived at Augsburg, the cardinal sent by the Pope received Luther with all civility. He made no doubt that he could soon settle this son of a German miner; and so perhaps he might, had he been the right man. But he took a high hand, and simply told him to withdraw his opposition and retract his words at once.

"What is wrong?" asked Luther.

The cardinal refused to discuss matters.

"I am come to command, not to argue," he replied.

But the little monk refused to retract.

Then, history says, the cardinal grew angry.

"What!" he cried. "What! Do you think the Pope cares for the opinion of a German peasant? The Pope's little finger is stronger than all Germany. Do you expect princes to defend you? I tell you, No; and where will you be then?"

"Then, as now, in the hands of Almighty God," answered Luther.

Then cardinal and monk parted. But Luther was too deeply moved to keep silent.

"God hurries and drives me," he said. "I am not master of myself. I wish to be quiet and am hurried into the midst of tumults."

At this moment Charles V became Emperor of Germany and ruler of half the world. Matters were now referred to him, for Luther was taking firmer ground and attacking not only the abuses of the papacy, but the whole Church of Rome.

At last, a command came from the Pope forbidding Luther to preach any more. He replied by burning the document at the gate of the city. Crowds gathered to see the fire blaze up. Then Luther, pale as death, stepped forward holding in his hand the document with the Pope's seal upon it. He knew full well what he was doing now as he dropped it into the flames that rose high that wintry afternoon at Wittenberg. The crowds shouted approval and admiration.

"It was the shout of the awakening of nations," says a famous writer. Not only the little crowd at Wittenberg, but the whole world, was looking on. For that little fire lit up the whole of Europe. Luther was now ordered by the Emperor Charles to appear before a council, or Diet, as it was called, which should meet at

Worms, a city on the Rhine. He was warned by his friends not to go, for feeling ran high. There would surely be bloodshed, they told him, and he would never leave Worms alive.

"Were there as many devils in Worms as there are tiles upon the roofs of the houses, I would go on," replied Luther.

The whole country was moved by his heroism. Whether he was right or whether he was wrong, this was a brave man. In April 1521, at ten in the morning, he arrived at Worms in the covered wagon provided for him.

"God will be with me," he said as he descended from the wagon.

Crowds assembled to see him as he passed to the council chamber, this resolute little monk, who was defying the Pope of Rome.

Inside, the scene was most impressive. On a raised platform sat Charles V, ruler of half the world. Archbishops, ministers, princes, stood on either side to hear and judge this son of a miner who had made the world ring with his name. In the body of the hall stood knights and nobles, stern hard men in gleaming armor. Between them Luther was led, still in his monk's dress. As he passed up the hall a knight touched him on the arm.

"Pluck up thy spirit, little monk," he said. "Some of us here have seen warm work in our time, but never knight in this company more needed a stout heart than thou needest it now. If thou hast faith, little monk, go on; in the name of God, forward!"

"Yes," said Luther, throwing back his head, "in the name of God, forward!"

At last he stood alone before his judges. The books he had written lay on a table at hand. The titles were read aloud, and he was asked if he had written them.

"Yes," was his firm answer.

Would he withdraw all he had written? No—that was impossible. For two long hours Luther defended his opinions. He would retract nothing. They might kill him if they wished, and he knew death was the penalty, but he was ready to die in such a cause. What he said he now repeated, for the matter had gone far beyond the sale of indulgences by this time.

"Here I stand. I cannot act otherwise. So help me God!"

Uttering these famous words, he ended.

The council broke up in excitement, and Luther was free to go home.

"It is past! It is past!" he cried in heartrending accents, as he clasped his hands above his head.

The verdict was not long in coming. It was against him. He must preach no more, teach no more. The emperor of half the world must uphold the authority of the Pope.

"Be it so," said Luther, uncomplaining. "I will bear any-thing for his Imperial Majesty and the Empire, but the Word of God must not be bound."

For the next year he was sheltered by one of his friends in an old German castle, lest he should suffer violence from the hands of those who disapproved his conduct. There he worked a great labor by translating the Bible into his native German. But after a time he returned to Wittenberg,—the scene of his old labors,—while others carried on the work of reformation which he had begun.

SIR THOMAS MORE, AD 1535

GEORGE HODGES

Sir Thomas More was the most eminent man of his time in England. He was known all over Europe for his scholarship and his statesmanship. But the most interesting thing about him for us is the fact that he represented, better than anybody else, the mind of many wise and good men who were in sympathy with the new ideas which were at that time beginning to change the world, and yet in sympathy also with the old ways. He was the intimate friend of Erasmus, who was the leader of such men in Europe.

More and Erasmus saw clearly that the Church of their day ought to be reformed. They felt, for example, very much as Luther felt about indulgences. They knew that religion, among many people, had come to be a matter of magic, a belief that saints and relics could save them from the punishment of their sins, and from the diseases of their bodies, and could bring them good luck both in this world and in the next. And they knew that religion among many priests, had come to be a matter of money; all that they cared for was to be rich. They desired to have these evils stopped. Thus they were in sympathy with the reforms which had been started by Luther. But, at the same time, they cared greatly for the Church. They saw that along with all that was wrong, there was much more that was right. And this they wished to keep. They feared that the Reformation would go too far. When they found that Luther, having attacked the indulgences, had proceeded to attack the pope who permitted them, and having defied the pope, had denied the necessity of the sacraments from which the pope had excommunicated him, they felt that he was like a man, who, finding a wasps' nest under the eaves of his house, burns out the nest with so great a fire that he burns the whole house with it.

Thus in a time when all the world was taking sides, some Protestant and others Catholic, some for the new and others for the old, More and Erasmus and such moderate men found themselves in a difficult position. They were on both sides, and on neither.

One time, while Henry the Seventh was the king, More, though he was but twenty-four years of age, was a member of Parliament; and the king demanded of the House of Commons a great sum of money, much more than he had any right to ask; and when the House was silent, being unwilling to vote the money, and yet unwilling to offend the king, More made a speech the effect of which was to give the king very much less than he had required. Some of the king's people told him that he had been defeated by a beardless boy. Coming thus under the ill-will of the king, he retired into private life. And there the debate between what was called the old learning and the new occupied his thoughts. At first, he studied Greek and science, like a man of the new time. Then he gave himself to devotion and prayer in a monastery, and planned to be a priest, like a man of the old time. The matter was happily decided for the moment by a visit which he made to Mr. Colt's house, in Essex, where he met his daughter Jane and married her[79]. But it illustrates the contention in his mind between the new and the old.

Then the seventh Henry died, and the eighth Henry came to the throne, and More came out of his retirement into great favor. He was made a member of the Privy Council, and Treasurer of the Exchequer, and was chosen Speaker of Parliament. The new king so delighted in his conversation that More could hardly get leave to go home from the court to his own family as much as once a month. The king would send for him to come to his private room, and there would talk with him sometimes

---

79   A married person cannot be a monk.

about this world, sometimes about the next, and then would take him to the palace roof on clear nights, "there to consider with him the diversities, courses, motions, and operations of the stars and planets." And when More, tiring of this and desiring to go home, would stay away from court, the king would visit him in his own house, coming to dinner without being invited, and afterwards walking with More in the garden by the hour together with his arm about his neck.

William Roper, More's son-in-law, who wrote a biography of his life, congratulated him on this royal friendship. But More said, "Son Roper, I may tell thee I have no cause to be proud thereof; for if my head would win him a castle in France, it should not fail to go."

By-and-by, he was made Lord Chancellor[80]; his father, in the meantime, being only a judge of the Court of the King's Bench. It is remembered that as Sir Thomas passed through Westminster Hall, he would often go into his father's court, and reverently kneel down and ask his father's blessing; and that when he and his father met in any place, "notwithstanding his high office, he would offer the pre-eminence to his father."

More became Lord Chancellor by reason of the fall of Cardinal Wolsey; and the fall of Cardinal Wolsey was occasioned by the difficulties connected with the king's divorce.

---

80   Highest government position under the king.

Henry the Eighth had married Catherine, his brother's widow, daughter of Ferdinand and Isabella of Spain. They had lived happily together, but their marriage had been saddened by the death of their children. Child after child died in infancy; only a daughter, Mary, lived. There was no son to follow Henry on the throne. Moreover, as one child after another died, Henry began to fear that he was being punished for a marriage which many good men believed to be against the will of God. These people thought it was wrong for a man to marry his deceased brother's wife. Then Henry fell in love with a young lady of the court, named Anne Boleyn.

Thus the rights and wrongs of the matter were very complicated. It was clearly right for Henry to regret leaving the succession to the throne in such doubt that there would probably be a war between different claimants. It was clearly wrong for Henry to fall in love with Anne Boleyn. As for the divorce which he desired from Catherine, some said one thing, and some another. Anyhow, it became Wolsey's business to secure the divorce by getting the permission of the pope. And in this he failed. In the changes of power in Europe, Italy and the pope came under the rule of Spain, and the pope would not venture to do a thing so offensive to Spain as to allow the divorce of the daughter of Ferdinand and Isabella. Thus Wolsey fell into disgrace, and his chancellorship was given to Sir Thomas More.

Then Henry decided to proceed with the divorce in spite of the pope. He followed Luther's example. The pope said to Luther, "You are excommunicated; you are from henceforth forbidden to partake of the sacraments of the Church." Luther answered, "That will make no difference to me. I shall suffer no loss by your refusal of the sacraments: they do not depend on Church approval." The pope said to Henry, "You may not be divorced. I refuse to give you my permission." Henry answered, "That will make no difference to me. You claim to be a ruler in my kingdom, and to enforce your laws, not only in the Church but in the state. I deny the claim. You are dismissed. From this day forward you are no ruler here. I do not care for your permission. I shall do precisely as I please."

Meanwhile, the Lord Chancellor had been attending, with all diligence, to the duties of his office. Every morning he sat from eight until eleven to hear cases, and every afternoon he was to be found in his house to hear petitions. Whoever had a grievance might bring it to his notice, and the poorer the suppliant the better. In a day when the taking of bribes was a common sin of judges, More declined all gifts. One time, his enemies, — for a great man in that age always had enemies, — declared that he had received a "fair great gilt cup" from a man in whose favor he had decided a case. And More confessed that the man's wife brought him the golden cup as a New Year's gift, and that he took it.

"There, gentlemen," cried the chief accuser, "did I not tell you that you should find this matter true?" Thereupon More answered that having received the cup at the lady's hands, he caused his butler to fill it with wine, and drank to her good health, and gave it back. "Thus was this great mountain turned scarce unto a mole-hill."

One time, the Duke of Norfolk, coming to dine with the Lord Chancellor, found him at the parish church in the midst of the service, with a surplice on his back, singing in the choir. After the service, as they went home arm in arm, the Duke said, "Well, well! My Lord, a parish clerk! A parish clerk! You dishonor the king and his office."

To which the Chancellor replied, smiling, "Your Grace may not think that the king, your master and mine, will be offended with me for serving God, his Master."

At a little distance from his mansion house, More built a place which contained a chapel and a library; and to this building he was accustomed to go that he might be alone to read and pray; and especially on Fridays, he spent the whole day there, in his devotions, saying the seven penitential psalms and the litany and other prayers. This he found time to do, even in the midst of the great business of his high office, feeling that the essential thing, above all else, is that a man be the master of himself. Thus he kept on the watch against temptations.

Meanwhile, the matter of the king's divorce was coming forward. More was against it. He believed that the pope was right in refusing to allow it. When he perceived that the matter was decided, he resigned his office. Out he went from his high place, a poor man as he had entered it. He called his children and his grandchildren together, who were all living with him in his great house, and said that he must now reduce his expenses.

"I have been brought up," he said, "at Oxford, at an Inn of Chancery, at Lincoln's Inn, and in the King's Court. Thus I have gone from the lowest degree to the highest. Now we must go back. We will begin with Lincoln's Inn diet, and live like the prosperous lawyers; and the next year, if we are not able to maintain this, we will go one step down to the Town Inn fare, and live like the less prosperous lawyers. If that exceed our ability too, then will we the next year after descend to Oxford fare, and live like scholars. Which, if our ability stretch not to maintain neither, then may we yet, with bags and wallets, go a-begging together, and so still keep company merrily." Thus he met his change of fortune with all cheerfulness.

While he was Lord Chancellor, one of his gentlemen, when the church service was over, was accustomed to go to his wife's pew, and say, "Madam, my Lord is gone," and thus escort her from the church. The day after he resigned his office, Sir Thomas himself came down after the service and standing by the pew made a low bow, saying, "Madam, my Lord is gone."

The king, however, was not contented with More's resignation. Chancellor or not, More was the greatest man in England, and his silence meant that he did not approve of the king's conduct. He refused to attend the coronation of Anne Boleyn. It was plain that he was opposed to the king's marriage. Thus he made an enemy of Anne and of the king. One time, he asked his daughter how Queen Anne did, and how things went at court. She answered, "Never better; there is nothing else but dancing and sporting." "Alas, Meg," said More, "it pitieth me to remember to what misery, poor soul, she will shortly come." Some say that he added, "These dances of hers will prove such dances that she will spurn off our heads like footballs."

Then the Act of Supremacy was passed, declaring the king head of the Church in England, in the pope's place. And first the clergy, and then the great men of the realm, were called upon to accept it.

"Mr. More," said the Duke of Norfolk, his good friend, "it is perilous striving with princes, and therefore I would wish you to incline somewhat to the king's pleasure."

"Is that all, my Lord?" said More. "Is there, in good faith, no more difference between your Grace and me, but that I shall die today and you tomorrow?"

Thus he went to appear before the Lords at Lambeth. That morning, as his custom was when he entered into any matter of importance, he went first to church and said his prayers. It was also his custom, whenever he went away from home, to have his wife and children come with him to his boat, and there to kiss them all and bid them farewell; but that morning he would not let them come, but shut the gate behind him.

Presently, in the boat, he said to William Roper, "Son Roper, I thank the Lord, the field is won."

Roper answered, "Sir, I am thereof very glad."

But as he considered what more meant, it became plain that he had thanked the Lord that He had enabled him to go forward in obedience to what his conscience called him to do, in spite of his great love of his family. When he shut the gate, he knew that for conscience sake he was shutting himself out from his pleasant home, from all the joys of his delightful life, and from the sight of the loved faces of his wife and children.

Thus More refused to take the oath of supremacy as against his conscience, and they put him in prison in the Tower. There he remained for more than a year, in the hardship of close confinement, deprived of even books and paper.

One time, when his wife came to see him, being a simple

person, and not understanding these great matters, she remonstrated with him. "What the good year, Mr. More," said she, "I marvel that you, that have been always hereunto taken for so wise a man, will now so play the fool to lie here in this close, filthy prison, and be content to be shut up among mice and rats, when you might be abroad at your liberty, and with the favor and good-will both of the king and his Council, if you would but do as all the bishops and best learned of this Realm have done. And seeing you have at Chelsea a right, fair house, your library, your books, your gallery, your orchards, where you might, in the company of me your wife, your children, and household, be merry, I muse what in God's name you mean here still fondly to tarry."

To whom Sir Thomas, having listened quietly with a cheerful countenance said, "I pray thee, tell me, tell me one thing."

"What is that," said she.

"Is not this house as nigh heaven as mine own?"

To whom she, after her accustomed fashion, not liking much talk, answered, "Tilly vally, tilly vally!"

But his daughter Margaret understood him better. With her he said the psalms and the litany, as he had been wont to do at family prayers at home. "I find no cause, I thank God, Meg," he said, "to reckon myself in worse case here, than in mine own house." And Margaret's husband, William Roper, writing the story of his life, adds the comment, "Thus by his gracious demeanor in tribulations appeared it, that all the troubles that ever chanced unto him, by his patient sufferance thereof were to him no painful punishments, but of his patience profitable exercises."

At last, being brought to trial, the solicitor-general[81], Rich, recounted a conversation which he claimed to have had with More.

"Admit that there were, sir, an Act of Parliament, that all the Realm should take me for the king, would not you, Mr. More, take me for the king?"

"Yes, sir," said More, "that would I."

"I put the case further, that there were an Act of Parliament that all the Realm should take me for the pope, would then not you, Mr. More, take me for the pope?"

"For answer," said Sir Thomas, "to your first case, the Parliament may well, Mr. Rich, meddle with the state of temporal princes; but to make answer to your second case, I will put you this case: Suppose the Parliament would make a law, that God should not be God, would you then, Mr. Rich, say God were not God?"

"No, sir," said he, "that would I not, since no parliament may make any such law."

---

81   Chief legal officer in England.

"No more," said Sir Thomas, according to Rich's report, "could the Parliament make the king the supreme head of the Church."

This was the sole evidence against him, and this More denied. But his death had been determined. The king was not willing that there should live, even in silence, a man whose disapproval was a constant criticism upon him.

Thus he was condemned to die. And as he came, after his condemnation, from Westminster to the Tower, his daughter Margaret was waiting by the way to see him. And she, "pressing in amongst the midst of the throng and the company of the guard, that with halberds and bills were round about him, hastily ran to him, and there, openly in the sight of them all, embraced and took him about the neck and kissed him, who, well liking her most daughterly love and affection towards him, gave her his fatherly blessing, and many godly words of comfort besides; from whom after she was departed, she not satisfied with the former sight of her dear father, giving respect neither to herself, nor to the press of the people and multitudes that were about him, suddenly turned back again, and ran to him as before, took him about the neck, and divers times together most lovingly kissed him, and at last with a full heavy heart was fain to depart from him; the beholding whereof was, to many of them that were present thereat, so lamentable, that it made them for very sorrow to mourn and weep."

Sir Thomas More was beheaded on the seventh day of July, 1535. The scaffold was poorly built, and as he and the lieutenant of the Tower climbed the steps together, he said, "I pray you, I pray you, Mr. Lieutenant, see me safe up, and for my coming down, let me shift for myself." Thus he died, composed and with a cheerful face, kneeling down and commending his soul to God in whom he put his trust, and whose obedience he valued above all the pleasures of his life.

When the Emperor Charles heard of this tragedy, he called the English ambassador, and said, "My Lord Ambassador, we understand that the king, your master, hath put his faithful servant and grave wise councilor, Sir Thomas More, to death." The ambassador answered that the circumstances were unknown to him. "Well," said the emperor, "it is very true, and this we will say, that if we had been master of such a servant, we would rather have lost the best city of our dominions, than such a worthy councilor."

JOHN BUNYAN,
AD 1688

GEORGE HODGES

John Bunyan was brought up in Puritan England. In Bedford, where he lived, the prevailing religion was of the Puritan kind. His father, indeed, was a tinker, and the boy was taught that trade; and the tinkers were wandering people, like gypsies, who went about from village to village mending pots and kettles and doing odd jobs, and were not much interested in religion. The elder Bunyan, however, seems to have stayed in Beford; being in that respect unlike most tinkers. And the younger Bunyan, from his earliest youth, was singularly sensitive to religious influences.

The Puritan religion laid great emphasis upon the fact of sin. The Puritans were Calvinists, and believed that all people are born fallen, and are under the wrath of God, unless they escape. Some are enabled to escape, by the grace of God, through the mercy gained for sinners by the death of Christ. Salvation

Printed for Nat. Ponder in the Poultrey.

THE
Pilgrim's Progreſs
FROM
THIS WORLD,
TO
That which is to come

Delivered under the Similitude of a

DREAM

Wherein is Diſcovered,
The Manner of his ſetting out,
His Dangerous JOURNEY,
AND
Safe Arrival at the Deſired Countrey.

By *JOHN BUNYAN.*

The Third Edition, with Additions.

I have uſed Similitudes, *Hoſea*, 12. 10.

Licenſed and Entred according to Order.

LONDON,
Printed for *Nath. Ponder,* at the *Peacock*
in the *Poultrey* near *Cornhil,* 1679.

was thought to be a matter of much uncertainty and difficulty. Every sin strengthened its hold. Before John Bunyan was ten years old, he dreamed night after night that the devil was running away with him.

It is indeed true that life is a serious matter, and that sin is a grievous thing, and that we must be on guard against temptation, and that nothing is so important as right thinking, and right speaking, and right acting. It is true that we must, above all things, do our duty, and heed the voice of conscience. But it is true also that the world is very pleasant, that the sun shines and the birds sing, and that God has given us not only souls but bodies. It is true that God has implanted in us the desire not only to pray but to play, and that we naturally laugh more than we cry because we are made that way.

So there was young John Bunyan, with a strong love for dancing with the girls on the village green, and for joining with the boys in ringing the bells of the village church. He liked to play tip-cat[82]. There was even a novel which he liked to read, called the "History of Sir Bevis of Southampton," a story of knights and ladies and adventures. But as he did these pleasant things, there was in his soul an unhappy feeling that he was doing wrong. One bad habit he certainly had: he was given to swearing. But even this seems to have been a kind of natural

---

82   A game played by hitting a small stick, "the cat," with a larger stick or bat.

protest against the sober piety about him. Whatever was the reason for it, he stopped it when he was rebuked and told how wrong it was.

Thus he lived up to the age of seventeen, a good lad, saying his prayers and reading his Bible, and listening every Sunday to very long sermons, terribly afraid of the devil, and imagining himself—poor little fellow—to be a great sinner. Then King Charles gathered his army together to fight for what he believed to be his rights, and the parliament gathered an army against him, and the civil war began, and Bunyan became a soldier.

He brought out of this experience a knowledge of battles which he never forgot. The drums and trumpets, the flying banners, the discipline of the camp, the shock of the charge, the noise of guns, the sight of blood and death, illustrated that war which the devil is forever waging against the soul of man. He brought also a new sense of the uncertainty of life. At the siege of a city, one of his companions, who had for the moment taken Bunyan's place, was killed.

He came back out of the wars, and married a wife whose only dowry was a bundle of religious books. These he read, and the reading quickened[83] all his former uneasiness about his sins. One day in the midst of a game of tip-cat, he heard a voice

83   To come to life.

in his soul demanding whether he would leave his sins and go to heaven, or continue in his sins and go to hell. There he stood with his stick uplifted in his hand, staring at the sky. He never played again. He gave up bellringing, though he looked on while the other young men pulled the ropes, till he was suddenly seized with an awful fear that the steeple would fall upon his head. He gave up dancing on the green.

For a time, his religious scruples gave him such distress that he seemed in danger of losing his mind. He thought that he had committed the unpardonable sin, though he did not know exactly what it was. He thought that if he had faith, even as a grain of mustard seed, he could dry up all the puddles between Elstow and Bedford. He was assailed day after day with a temptation to sell Christ84. Wherever he went, and whatever he did, he heard the devil at his ear whispering, "Sell him. Sell him." At last he cried, "Let him go if he will"; and then he thought that he was lost indeed. Even after these agonies were over, and he began to come out of this valley of the shadow of death, and joined the Baptist church at Bedford, and partook, for the first time, of the Lord's Supper, he was tempted to shock the congregation by swearing aloud. And after he had begun to preach, he felt the devil urging him to say horribly wicked

---

84   Bunyan was tempted to abandon or "sell" Christ for worldly things like pleasure, comfort, and wealth.

things in the midst of his sermons. Out of these spiritual torments he was brought at last into peace and joy by the suffering of real pain. He was arrested and put in jail at Bedford and kept there for twelve years.

For Cromwell was now gone, and his son Richard, who for a while reigned in his stead, was not strong enough to govern England, and so Charles the Second was invited to come back and take the throne from which his father had been thrust out. And when the king came back the Church came with him. During Cromwell's time all the ministers in England were Puritans, and all the services were Puritan services. Even in the cathedrals, the prayers of the ministers took the place of the ancient prayers of the book. The Episcopal clergy, who had been turned out of their churches in Queen Mary's time by the Roman Catholics, were now turned out by Presbyterians and Congregationalists. But the king came back, and at once all was changed. It was now the Presbyterians and the Congregationalists who must go. All who were willing to use the prayer-book might remain, but a law was passed that after a certain Sunday, all who were not willing to do that must resign their places. Accordingly, a great many Puritan ministers resigned, nearly two thousand. And not only that, but other laws were passed to prevent them from preaching. For the moment, in the enthusiasm of the return of the king and of the Church, the plans of Laud were taken up again, and it was proposed to compel everybody in England to belong to the Episcopal Church.

Thus when John Bunyan, in defiance of the laws, began to preach without having the permission of a bishop, he was put in jail. The authorities felt that if they allowed uneducated and unordained men to preach, the confusion of the time would be continued. The old order had returned to power, and was putting down the new liberty. They tried to get the tinker to promise that he would not preach; but he felt like the apostles that he was sent from God and must preach, no matter what the laws might be. To jail he went, then.

They laughed at him; they said that the only divine commission which he had was to mend old kettles. They threatened him. "If you break the law," they said, "you will be banished, and if you come back, we will hang you by the neck." Nothing could make Bunyan promise not to preach. "If you let me out to-day," he said, "I will preach again tomorrow."

So there he lay in jail. Jails, even now, are not comfortable places. In Bunyan's time they were hot in summer and bitterly cold in winter, and filthy all the year round. Moreover, being in jail, he was not only separated from his family, but was unable to support them by working at his trade. He knew that his wife and his little children, whom he dearly loved, were hungry because he would not promise not to preach.

319

He thought of his blind daughter, how she had no food and no fire. Even this did not change his resolution. He knew that God commanded him to preach, and preach he would. "I must," he said, "I must do it."

Unable to ply his trade of tinker, Bunyan learned in his prison to make "long-tagged thread laces," and sold them. And he preached to his companions in captivity, making the jail a church for those who were confined in it with him. And as he worked, he read. He had two books, the Bible and Foxe's "Book of Martyrs." These he read over and over, till he knew them almost by heart. And presently, he began to write. He was a poor speller, and his grammar was tinker's grammar, but he had certain advantages which more than made up for these defects.

One of his advantages was an earnest spirit. He wrote solely for the purpose of helping his neighbors, and with as little thought for his own fame or gain as any of the prophets or apostles. He believed that God wished him to preach, and being hindered from preaching with his voice, he preached with his pen. Another of his advantages was an acquaintance with his own soul, and with the souls of other poor people like himself. He had gone through a deep religious experience and had come out of darkness into light, and thus knew the way and was able to be a guide.

Still another advantage was his intimate familiarity with the greatest of all books; for the best education consists in part of experience of life, and in part of knowledge of the thoughts of great thinkers. Bunyan, reading the Bible day and night, learning by heart its history and poetry, associating continually with its sages and saints, and breathing in its divine spirit, was better educated in Bedford jail than any youth of the time who was studying Latin and Greek at Oxford. Thus he wrote the deep thoughts of his own soul in the language of the Bible. Even his imprisonment helped him, for he had time to think and write.

In jail at Bedford, then, this poor tinker began the book which made him famous. "As I walked through the wilderness of this world," he said, "I lighted on a certain place where was a den, and laid me down in that place to sleep." The den was Bedford jail. "And as I slept," he says, "I dreamed a dream. I dreamed, and behold, I saw a man clothed with rags standing in a certain place, with his face from his own house, a book in his hand, and a great burden upon his back. I looked and saw him open the book and read therein; and not being able longer to contain he broke out with a lamentable cry, saying, 'What shall I do?'" Thus begins the Pilgrim's Progress.

The man, whose name was Christian, answered his own question by making his way out of the City of Destruction where he dwelt, and taking his journey through all manner of hindrances and perils to the land of Beulah, and the Mount Zion, and the Celestial City, the heavenly Jerusalem. He tumbled into the Slough of Despond, but struggled out again. He got into trouble by following the advice of Mr. Worldly Wiseman, but was brought back by the aid of the Evangelist. He learned useful lessons in the House of the Interpreter. He came upon a cross beside the way, and the burden of his sins fell off. From the heights of the Hill Difficulty, he saw in the far distance, in the midst of Immanuel's Land, the fair slopes of the Delectable Mountains. He did hard but successful battle with the dragon Apollyon, and entered into the Valley of the Shadow of Death. "I thought over and over," he says, "I should have been killed there; but at last the day broke, and the sun rose." He passed the tower of Vanity Fair. In the grounds of Doubting Castle he lay down to sleep, and Giant Despair came out and got him. The Giant put him in a dungeon and beat him with a grievous crab-tree cudgel. At last, says Christian, "What a fool am I thus to lie in an evil-smelling dungeon, when I may as well walk at liberty. I have a key in my bosom, called Promise, that will, I am persuaded, open any lock in Doubting Castle." So out he came, and reached the Delectable Mountains, and came in sight of the Celestial City. He forded a deep river which lay before Mount Zion, and in the shining city all the bells began to ring, and over the gate was written, "Blessed are they that do his commandments that they may have right to the tree of life, and may enter in through the gates into the city."

And the gates opened, and Christian entered; and "I looked in," says he who dreamed the dream, "and behold, the city shone like the sun; the streets also were paved with gold; and in them walked many men, with crowns on their heads, palms in their hands, and golden harps, to sing praises withal. And after that, they shut up the gates; which, when I had seen, I wished myself among them."

The Pilgrim's Progress came into the hands of people who were hungry for good stories, as all right-minded people are, but who had persuaded themselves that stories are bad reading. They had denied themselves the pleasant company of Sir Bevis of Southampton and of all the other heroes of romance. As for Shakespeare, his wonderful stories were worse than the others because they were plays and the Puritans associated plays with all wickedness. Thus even children, in those days, were growing up without knowing what the delight of stories meant. They had, it is true, the Bible in which were the most marvelous stories which were ever told; but the Bible stories were told so soberly and with so little thought that any child would ever read them that most of the children found them as difficult as the long Sunday sermons. But here, at last, was a book of pious stories, yet not so pious as to be uninteresting; a book about giants and dragons, and adventurous heroes, a fairy tale, which could be read even by Puritans, and even on Sunday!

At first, only poor people read it, Bunyan's neighbors in Bedford and Elstow, and other uneducated persons. It was printed on coarse paper, with queer, cheap pictures. But the fame of it passed from one to another. There was a second edition, a third, an eighth, a ninth, a tenth. Even before Bunyan died, many thousand copies had been sold, in England, in Scotland, even in France and Holland, even across the ocean in the Puritan colonies. Bunyan wrote a second part, in which Christian's wife and children journeyed over the same road. Other books came from his pen; the Holy Way, an account of the siege of the soul; Grace Abounding, an account of his own religious life. But Pilgrim's Progress stands by itself as not only the best of Bunyan's writings, but as the most popular religious book ever written in the English language.

Bunyan was released from jail and became so eminent a person that he was called "the bishop of the Baptists." Charles the Second wished for various reasons to favor the Roman Catholics, and he repealed the laws which punished those who would not attend the service of the Church of England. By this repeal all the other dissenters benefited. All the jails were opened, and they who had been convicted, like Bunyan, of having "devilishly and perniciously abstained from coming to church," were set free. Now he might preach as much as he liked. And preach he did, even in London, and in a hundred country towns. One time he went in a pouring rain to persuade an angry father to forgive a disobedient son and caught a heavy cold of which he died. His grave in Bunhill Fields became a Protestant shrine and place of pilgrimage. His supreme sermon was his great book, in which he lives and preaches still.

JOHN WESLEY, AD 1791

GEORGE HODGES

John Wesley had fourteen brothers and sisters. One time, after he had become a man, he asked his mother to write out some of the methods which she had used in bringing up her large family, and her reply he copied in his journal. She taught her children, when they were punished, to cry softly, "by which means they escaped abundance of correction they might otherwise have had." They were so constantly accustomed to eat and drink what was set before them, whether they liked it or not, that there was no difficulty in making them take medicine: "they durst not refuse it." Mrs. Wesley said that "in order to form the minds of children, the first thing to be done is to conquer their will and bring them to an obedient temper." As soon as they could speak, they were taught the Lord's Prayer, which they said at rising and at bedtime, and "they were very early made to distinguish the Sabbath from other days." Every act of obedience, "especially when it crossed upon their own inclinations," was commended and rewarded. All property rights were very carefully observed. No child was "suffered to invade the property of another in the smallest matter, though it were but of the value of a farthing, or a pin." Every day the older children read aloud to the younger the Psalms for the day, out of the prayer-book, and a chapter of the Old Testament in the morning, and of the New Testament in the evening.

In this orderly household Wesley passed his early years. His father was a clergyman of the Church of England, and he was to follow in his steps. The life was strict and sober, but the children enjoyed themselves so much the more. They were very merry. It is remembered of John that he was "happy and sprightly, with a turn for wit and humor."

In due time he went to college at Oxford and entered the ministry at the age of twenty-two. Part of his time he spent as an assistant in his father's parish, where he "read plays, attended the village fairs, shot plovers[85] in the fenlands, and enjoyed a dance with his sisters," and perhaps with some who were not his sisters; besides attending to his more serious duties. But his chief interest was in the university. He was made a teacher of Greek there, and had a group of students about him whom he tutored.

---

85   A type of bird.

All this time, religion was as natural to Wesley as eating and drinking. He was in no way disturbed by it, nor was he very earnestly concerned about it. His conscience did not trouble him. He was determined, however, to make the most of himself. He kept a diary in which he set down how he used his time; having his hours and tasks very carefully arranged, — this he would do at eight, and that at nine, and so on through the day. He began to read books of devotion, especially the writings of Thomas à Kempis. He gradually gathered about him a little company of Oxford men who agreed to spend their evenings together. On weekdays they read the classics aloud, and on Sundays the Greek Testament. More and more, the life of religion seemed to these young men to be the supreme thing. They made rules for themselves, fasting on Wednesdays and Fridays, and going to the Holy Communion every Sunday. One day they heard about a man who was in the Oxford jail for killing his wife, and they went to visit him. That led to other visits to the prisoners. Presently, they began to go about among the poor, praying with them and reading the Bible.

This behavior attracted attention in the university. And, curiously enough, very few liked it. The young tutors and fellows were laughed at. Their little association was called the Godly Club, or the Holy Club. The men were called Methodists, because they kept the rules of the Church, and tried to live the life

329

of religion methodically. When they went to church, they found a crowd of students by the door waiting to jeer at them as they went in.

Wesley's enthusiasm led him to become a missionary. At that time, any zealous person who wished to do difficult mission work came to America. Thus Wesley took ship for Georgia, intending to devote himself to the conversion of the American Indians.

Among his companions on the sea were certain German emigrants who were of the Moravian religion. The early Moravians were disciples of John Hus. After many persecutions they had fled from Moravia, and a company of them had been invited by Count Zinzendorf to settle on his estates in Saxony. There they had built a town called Herrnhut. They had become a society in the Lutheran Church, as the Franciscans and the Jesuits were societies in the Roman Church. Out of Herrnhut these German emigrants had come, offering themselves for Christian work in Georgia. Now, on the voyage, there was a tremendous storm, and the wind split the mainsail, and the ship seemed likely to go down. but while most of the passengers were greatly excited and overcome with terror, the Moravians said their prayers with entire serenity of spirit and seemed quite ready to accept, with cheerfulness, whatever came, whether life or death. Wesley felt that they had something in their religion which he lacked.

They all arrived in Georgia safely, and Wesley was put in charge of the parish of Savannah. But the Indians were in the woods, and Wesley could not reach them. Even the English did not receive him with much satisfaction, for immediately he insisted on applying to the people there in the wilderness the rules which he and the Holy Club had kept at Oxford. He proposed to have all the provisions of the prayer-book observed strictly. He declared that infants must be baptized by immersion, because that method was given the preference in the book. He required that everybody who intended to come to the Holy Communion must give notice the day before, according to the book. And one young woman who had neglected to give such notice he repelled from the Lord's Table. Unhappily, this young woman had been so great a friend of Wesley's that he had asked her to marry him, and she had declined, and had married another. The young minister's action was laid to jealousy and anger. And all her friends were so indignant about it that Wesley thought it wise to bring his ministry in Savannah to a rather abrupt close. He suddenly departed from the town, and from the colony, and returned to England.

One of the complaints against Wesley was that he introduced new hymns into the service of the Church. He published, in Charleston, in 1737, a book of Psalms and Hymns, some of which he had translated from the German. It was the beginning of a new use of music in the eighteenth century for the stirring of religious emotion. The singing at revival meetings goes back for its origin to Wesley's book. The hymns of Charles Wesley contributed almost as much to the renewal of religion in England as the sermons of John.

Also, in Savannah, Wesley formed a society. He had in his congregation a company of devout persons who met together like the Holy Club at Oxford. They began and ended their meetings with singing and praying, and in the midst of these exercises they read the Bible and talked about it. It was the idea which was at the heart of the administration of the great movement which Wesley was soon to start—this assembly of like-minded persons to pray and sing and speak together directly and informally.

Wesley said, the year before he died, "I do not remember to have felt lowness of spirits for a quarter of an hour since I was born." His journal shows, however, that he returned from Georgia much depressed. He felt that he had made a failure of his ministry. On the return voyage there was another dangerous storm, and he remembered the Moravians. He doubted if he had ever in his life been a good Christian. He perceived that all his excellent doctrines, and his endeavors to grow in grace by means of the customs and sacraments of the Church, still left him cold. He seemed to himself like a house well-built, but neither warmed not lighted. Looking back over his ministry in later life, he said that thus far his labors bore no fruit, because at first, he "took for granted that all his hearers were believers and that many of them needed no repentance."

On the twenty-fourth of May, 1738, Wesley opened his Bible early in the morning, and looked to see what text would meet his eye, and it was St. Peter's saying about "great and precious promises."[86] In the afternoon, he attended the service at St. Paul's Cathedral, and was deeply impressed by the anthem, which was the psalm called De Profundis "Out of the deep have I called unto thee, Lord."[87] In the evening he went to a little devotional meeting where the speaker was discussing Martin Luther's Preface to the Epistle to the Romans. "About a quarter before nine," says Wesley, "while he was describing the change which God works in the heart through faith in Christ, I felt my heart strangely moved. I felt I did trust in Christ, Christ alone, for salvation, and an assurance was given me that He had taken away my sins, even mine, and saved me from the law of sin and death."

This experience was the beginning of a new kind of ministry. At first he preached in pulpits, but many of the regular ministers did not like what he said. And whether they liked it or

---

86   2 Peter 1:4
87   Psalm 130

not, the congregations were too big for the churches. He began to preach in the churchyards, and in the streets, and in the open fields. People came in thousands. Thus he went from one town to another. Early in his ministry he formed the habit of getting up every morning at four o'clock; and almost every day he preached at five. For years he traveled five thousand miles a year and preached fifteen sermons every week.

He had to have assistance, but he could not find ministers enough to help him. Some did not approve of him; some could not leave their parishes. He made preachers out of the people. Presently he had a hundred earnest men who had been converted by his preaching and were going out to preach to others. The movement extended out of England into Ireland, into Scotland, into America. It aroused the whole English-speaking people.

Wesley met with continual opposition. People hooted at him, and stoned him. Sometimes when he spoke in a churchyard, they rang the bells so that his voice could not be heard. In one place they drove a herd of cows in among the congregation as they stood in the street. In another place, "we came into town," says Wesley, "about eleven; and many people seemed very desirous to hear for themselves, concerning the way which is everywhere spoken against; but it could not be; the sons of Belial gathered themselves together, headed by one or two wretches called gentlemen; and continued shouting, cursing, blaspheming, and throwing showers of stones, almost without intermission. So that after some time spent in prayer for them, I judged it best to dismiss the congregation."

One time a mob beset the house where he was staying. "Bring out the minister!" they cried, "we will have the minister!" Wesley went out and "spoke a few words, which God applied," and they all cried with might and main, "The gentleman is an honest gentleman, and we will spill our blood in his defense." One day he writes in his journal, "To attempt speaking was vain, for the noise on every side was like the roaring of the sea; so they dragged me along till we came to the town, where seeing the door of a large house open, I attempted to go in; but a man, catching me by the hair, pulled me back into the middle of the mob. I broke out aloud into prayer. And now the man who had just before headed the mob, turned, and said, 'Sir, I will spend my life for you; follow me and not one soul here shall touch a hair of your head.'" And Wesley adds, "from the beginning to the end I found the same presence of mind as if I had been sitting in my own study."

Thus he preached day after day. His journal reads like the account in the Acts of the missionary journeys of St. Paul.

But there were attentive congregations, too. "In the midst of the sermon, a large cat, frightened out of a chamber, leaped down upon a woman's head, and ran over the heads and shoulders of many more; but none of them moved, or cried out, any more than if it had been a butterfly."

And in many places the results were such as were described among the miners of Kingswood. "Kingswood does not now, as it did a year ago, resound with cursing and blasphemy. It is no more filled with drunkenness and uncleanness, and the idle diversions that naturally lead thereto. It is no longer full of wars and fightings, of clamor and bitterness, of wrath and envyings: peace and love are there."

Wesley ministered not only to the souls but to the minds of the poor people. "No man in the eighteenth century did so much to create a taste for good reading, and to supply them with books at the lowest prices." This printing became a great business, and the money which Wesley made by it he used for the relief of poverty. He provided those who were in distress with clothes and food. He established lending offices for the help of struggling businessmen. To all these interests he brought his wonderful genius for organization. He changed the life of England.

All this time, the Methodists were a society in the English Church. Wesley would not allow them to hold their meetings at the hours when there was service in the parish churches. They were sent to the regular ministers for the sacraments.

But in America the Church of England had no bishops.

There was great need of supervision and nobody to supervise. And at last Wesley appointed men for the American work, who were at first called superintendents, but were soon called bishops. Wesley felt, indeed, that he was himself a bishop by the grace of God, as St. Paul was. But the final result was separation. During Wesley's life the Methodist societies continued in the Church, but when the end of his long labors came, the desire of the leading Methodists waited no longer. Out they came into independence.

Wesley lived through the hard days of opposition into a time when almost all men revered him. He was recognized in England as one who belonged with the saints and the apostles. One who knew him in those days said, "So fine an old man I never saw. The happiness of his mind beamed forth in his countenance." He might well be happy. He had served God with all his strength; he had saved souls; he had fought the good fight; he knew that there was laid up for him the crown of righteousness which is the reward of the faithful servants of God.

6. Church of Qualb-Luzeh in Syria. 4.—5. Cent.

Niceno-Constantinopolitan Creed
Commonly called the Nicene Creed

We believe in one God,
the Father, the Almighty,
maker of heaven and earth,
of all that is, seen and unseen.
We believe in one Lord, Jesus Christ,
the only Son of God,
eternally begotten of the Father,
God from God, Light from Light,
true God from true God,
begotten, not made,
of one Being with the Father.
Through him all things were made.
For us and for our salvation
he came down from heaven:
by the power of the Holy Spirit
he became incarnate from the Virgin Mary,
and was made man.
For our sake he was crucified under Pontius Pilate;
he suffered death and was buried.
On the third day he rose again
in accordance with the Scriptures;
he ascended into heaven
and is seated at the right hand of the Father.
He will come again in glory to judge the living and the dead,
and his kingdom will have no end.
We believe in the Holy Spirit, the Lord, the giver of life,
who proceeds from the Father and the Son.
With the Father and the Son he is worshiped and glorified.
He has spoken through the Prophets.
We believe in one holy catholic and apostolic Church.
We acknowledge one baptism for the forgiveness of sins.
We look for the resurrection of the dead,
and the life of the world to come. Amen.

Fig. 267   Church at Borgund.

WORKS EXCERPTED

SELECTIONS ARE FROM
THE FOLLOWING PUBLIC DOMAIN WORKS:

History of the Church for Children, John Mason Neale

Stories of Saints and Martyrs, Jetta Wolff

Stories of Saints for Children, Mrs. Molesworth

Life of Antony, St. Athanasius of Alexandria

Saints and Heroes to the End of the Middle Ages, George Hodges

Virgin Saints and Martyrs, Sabine Barring-Gould

Our Island Saints, Amy Steedman

Boy's Book of Battles, Eric Wood

Famous Men of the Middle Ages, John Haaren

Story of the Crusades, E.M. Wilmot-Buxton

Lives of the Saints for Children, Theodor Berthold

In God's Garden, Amy Steedman

Stories from French History, Lena Dalkeith

European Hero Stories, Eva March Tappan

The Awakening of Europe, M.B. Synge

Saints and Heroes Since the Middle Ages, George Hodges

www.ingramcontent.com/pod-product-compliance
Lightning Source LLC
Chambersburg PA
CBHW020432130626
46549CB00001B/98